chinese
pavilion

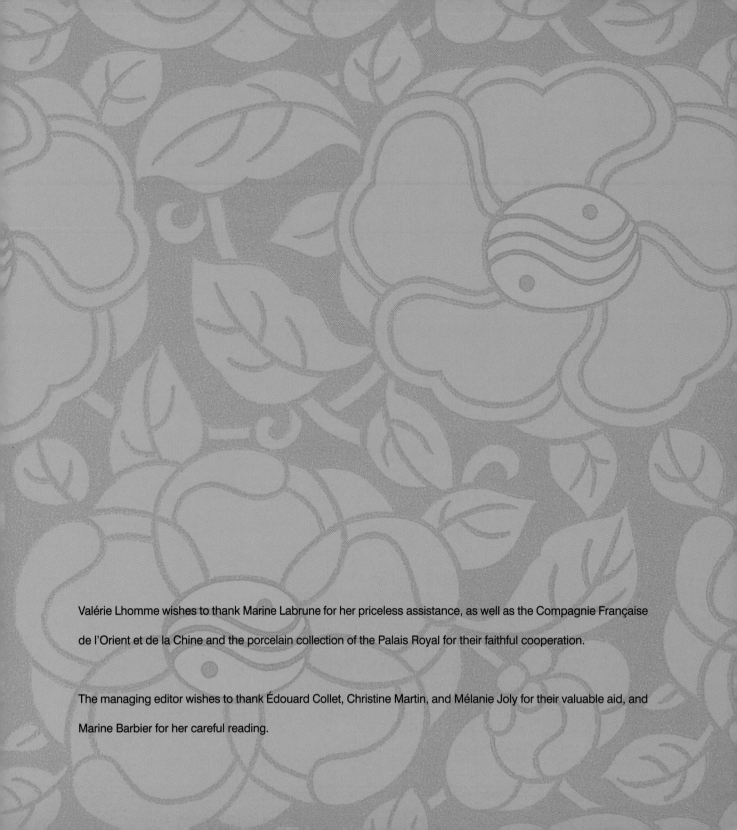

Valérie Lhomme wishes to thank Marine Labrune for her priceless assistance, as well as the Compagnie Française de l'Orient et de la Chine and the porcelain collection of the Palais Royal for their faithful cooperation.

The managing editor wishes to thank Édouard Collet, Christine Martin, and Mélanie Joly for their valuable aid, and Marine Barbier for her careful reading.

casual chinese cooking at home

chinese pavilion

Elisa Vergne

Photographs by Yves Bagros
Design by Valérie Lhomme

[When the flavors blend…]

To everyone's delight, national borders are slowly disappearing in matters of cuisine. As the new century gets underway, we're witnessing a gradual acceptance of new culinary habits. We don't talk about "exotic cuisine" anymore because exotic means faraway, strange, and not necessarily authentic. We no longer consider Chinese, Indian, or Mexican food to be unusual fare. The sources of inspiration for our cooking no longer matter as long as the results are delicious. It used to be that trying our hands at foreign cuisine was considered audacious, even daring, but today it's part of our everyday lives. Ingredients that, in the past, had to be tracked down with the skill of a detective, or brought back by travelling friends, are now available locally from the neighborhood supermarket or even our corner grocer. We are no longer intimidated by peculiar spices, mysterious jars, or unusual fruits—but, instead, we are learning how to use them. The world is coming to us, and its flavors are awakening in our kitchens. At the same time, we're discovering different ways of eating, as well as new dietary principles and eating habits from other countries. Our kitchens have become the melting pots for a natural blending of tastes; what was once quite curious is now so familiar, we forget that its origins are foreign.

This book doesn't present the cuisine of a nation, but rather the cuisine of a patchwork of provinces that once formed (and continue to form) a vast empire based on a powerful tradition nourished by peasant, aristocratic, and philosophical roots. Many recipes and ingredients are taken from Taoist nutrition, which has existed for more than two-thousand years. For a long time now, the rest of the world has been depending on the Chinese for a convenient solution to fast-paced modern living; Chinese takeouts are an established part of everyday life in both North America and Europe. However, more sophisticated, authentic recipes have also been finding their way into our homes. Many of us now have woks, convenient pans with a rounded base that allow us to stir-fry meat and vegetables to perfection and to fry foods in very little oil. Chinese cuisine has everything a person could desire: it's fast, rich in fresh and lively flavors, and low in calories. In addition, its basic ingredients are now easy to find, even if you live in a small town. And we're even starting to differentiate among regional traditions—Canton with its steamed dim sum, Shanghai with its pan-fried dumplings, Szechwan with its spicy dishes and sesame noodles, and Peking and northern China's glazed ducks, fondues, and steamed buns. The cuisine of the Chinese diaspora has also circled the globe, including chop suey and egg foo yung, both created in America. Discover, throughout the pages of this book, the most delicious classics of the Middle Empire.

contents

soups & salads

healthful soups

Chinese soups and broths are part of the ancient family of medicinal tonics and elixirs promoting long life in the Taoist tradition, as demonstrated by exotic ingredients, such as shark fins and birds' nests. These magic potions are thought to fortify and revitalize. Rather than serving as starters, they accompany the meal from start to finish.

Serves 4
Prep and cooking time:
10 minutes

1 stalk celery
Greens from 1 green onion
4 cups chicken stock (see
page 12)
2 eggs
Salt and pepper

[egg drop soup]

Rinse celery, remove any loose threads using a paring knife, and chop rest. Chop green onion stalk into fine rings (rinse well). In a pot, bring celery and stock to a boil.

Break eggs into a bowl and beat with a fork, then slowly pour into boiling stock while stirring constantly with a fork to make the "egg drops." Season with salt and pepper to taste.

Transfer soup to bowls and sprinkle with chopped onion greens.

[shrimp, cellophane noodle, and carrot salad]

Peel carrots and cut lengthwise into thin slices and then into strips. Peel cucumber section, cut in half, remove seeds, and cut rest into strips. Rinse celery stalks, remove threads with a paring knife, and cut into pieces about 1½ inches long and then into fine strips.

Cover noodles with boiling water and let soak for 3 minutes. Drain, rinse under cold water, drain again, and cut into pieces 1½ inches long using kitchen shears.

Beat eggs with a fork. In a nonstick frying pan, cook eggs (use some cooking spray) and then cut into strips. In a serving dish, mix carrots, cucumber, celery, and noodles.

Combine all the sauce ingredients and pour over contents of serving dish; combine. Sprinkle with cooked shrimp and egg strips, then snip chives over the salad.

Serves 4
Prep and cooking time:
30 minutes

2 small carrots
¼ cucumber
4 stalks celery
1 ounce cellophane (mung bean thread) noodles or thin rice noodles
2 eggs
⅓ pound peeled *cooked* shrimp
4 fresh chive spears

For the sauce:
3 tablespoons soy sauce
1 tablespoon peanut oil
1 teaspoon sesame seeds
2 tablespoons cider vinegar
1 teaspoon sugar
Pepper

[chicken stock]

Cut chicken into 8 pieces (or ask your butcher to do this). Peel garlic cloves and crush slightly. Peel ginger and slice. Rinse green onions and cut into pieces, including the greens.

In a narrow stockpot, slowly bring chicken to a boil in 3 quarts water.

As soon as water begins to boil, reduce heat and simmer, occasionally skimming off any foam that surfaces.

When the liquid is clear and no longer forms any foam, add garlic, ginger, green onions, and salt. Cover and simmer for at least 2 hours. Then strain stock and cool; remove fat from the top before using stock.

Makes 2 quarts
Prep time: 10 minutes
Cooking time: 2 hours 30 minutes

1 chicken (about 2 pounds)
4 cloves garlic
2-inch section fresh ginger
3 green onions
½ teaspoon salt

[shark fin soup]

Prepare shark fin according to the directions on the package or place in a saucepan of boiling water and cook for 1 hour. Rinse under cold water and soak in a pan of cold water for 14 hours, changing the water occasionally.

The next day, in a large pot, bring 2 quarts of water to a boil. Add whole chicken, drained shark fin, and salt; cover and simmer gently for 1 hour and 15 minutes.

Soak orange peel in lukewarm water for 15 minutes. Drain chicken. Place orange peel in stock, cover, and heat on very low.

Remove breast meat from chicken, discard the skin, and cut breast meat into small cubes. Add cubes to stock along with soy sauce and rice wine.

Stir cornstarch into 2 tablespoons cold water, pour into soup mixture, stir, and let thicken for 1 minute while stirring constantly.

Beat egg whites lightly with a fork, pour through a strainer into the soup and stir with chopsticks. Pour soup into a serving dish and sprinkle with chopped green onions.

If you find canned shark fin that's ready to use, simmer it for 15 minutes with 1/2 pound chicken breast in chicken stock (see page 12) seasoned with orange peel, soy sauce, and wine. Finish up by adding cornstarch and egg whites as described above.

Serves 6
Soaking time: 14 hours
Prep time: 20 minutes
Cooking time: 90 minutes

3 ounces dried shark fin
(specialty store)
1 chicken (about 2 pounds)
1 dried orange peel
2 tablespoons soy sauce
2 tablespoons rice wine
or sherry
1 tablespoon cornstarch
2 egg whites
3 whole, chopped
green onions
Salt

[chicken and wood ear mushroom soup]

Serves 4
Prep time: 15 minutes
Soaking time: 20 minutes
Marinating time: 20 minutes
Cooking time: 20 minutes

10 dried wood ear
mushrooms (or dried
shiitakes)
½ pound chicken breasts
2 tablespoons rice wine
or sherry
2 tablespoons soy sauce
Several drops sesame oil
1 teaspoon cornstarch
6 leaves Chinese (napa)
cabbage
5 cups chicken stock
(see page 12)
1 tablespoon peanut oil
⅓ pound peeled shrimp

Soak mushrooms in lukewarm water for 20 minutes. Dice chicken, mix with half the rice wine (or sherry), half the soy sauce, and all the sesame oil and cornstarch; let stand for 20 minutes at room temperature.

Rinse cabbage leaves and cut into strips. Rinse mushrooms, remove/discard stems, and slice caps finely. Drain diced chicken but save the marinade.

Heat stock. Add remaining soy sauce and rice wine along with mushrooms and chicken marinade. Simmer for 10 minutes (this forms the soup base).

In a frying pan, heat peanut oil and sear diced chicken and then sauté over high heat for 5 minutes or until cooked through. Remove from pan and drain on paper towels. Add cooked chicken and shrimp to soup and simmer for 5 minutes. Serve very hot.

[broccoli with oyster sauce]

Serves 4
Prep and cooking time:
10 minutes

1 pound broccoli
2 tablespoons oil
¼ cup oyster sauce
2 tablespoons rice wine
or sherry

Rinse broccoli under cold water and separate into small florets. Peel large stems and slice diagonally.

Drop broccoli florets and sliced stems into boiling water, turn off heat, and let stand for 2 minutes, then drain.

In a wok, heat oil and stir-fry broccoli for 2 minutes. Add oyster sauce and rice wine, stir-fry for another minute, and serve immediately. This goes well with rice.

[vegetable chop suey]

Soak the two types of mushroom separately in lukewarm water for 30 minutes. Rinse bamboo shoots. Rinse and drain bean sprouts. Peel carrot and cut into matchstick strips. Cut zucchini into matchstick strips. Remove stem and seeds from bell pepper, slice rest, and then cut into diamond shapes. Rinse green onions and slice finely from the white part into the green part. Separate broccoli into small florets.

Drain mushrooms and remove/discard stems from shiitakes. Slice caps of both types of mushroom. Heat oil and, one at a time, add carrot, zucchini, bell pepper, and white part of green onions while stirring constantly. Cook over medium-high heat for 5 minutes. Continue stirring and add broccoli, mushrooms, bamboo shoots, and bean sprouts.

Combine sugar and soy sauce and add to vegetables. Season with pepper. Stir and cook on very low for another 3–5 minutes. The vegetables should remain slightly crunchy. Sprinkle with the green part of the onions and serve while hot.

Serves 4
Prep and cooking time:
30 minutes
Soaking time: 30 minutes

4 dried wood ear
mushrooms
4 dried shiitake
mushrooms
¼ cup canned bamboo
shoots
¼ cup bean sprouts
(canned or fresh)
1 carrot
1 zucchini
1 bell pepper
2 green onions or
spring onions
½ pound broccoli
3 tablespoons oil
1 teaspoon sugar
2 tablespoons soy sauce
Pepper

注册　商标

Serves 4
Prep and cooking time:
15 minutes
Marinating time: 2–3 hours

1 Chinese (napa) cabbage
1–3 dried red chile peppers
(or 1 teaspoon crushed red
pepper flakes)
⅛ teaspoon ground pepper,
plus more to taste
¼ cup peanut oil
2 tablespoons sugar
2 tablespoons soy sauce
¼ cup rice wine vinegar
3 cloves garlic
1 tablespoon sesame oil
Salt

[chinese cabbage salad]

Cut cabbage into strips, submerge in boiling water, wait for water to return to a boil, and drain; place in a bowl or container. **S**auté chile peppers and pepper in hot peanut oil until the chiles turn brown. Strain oil over cabbage.

Dissolve sugar and 1 teaspoon salt in soy sauce and rice wine vinegar. Peel garlic, squeeze through a press, and add; then add sesame oil. Mix well and pour over cabbage; combine. Marinate covered in the refrigerator for 2–3 hours.

Just before serving, stir salad and drain; add more salt to taste if desired.

In Cantonese, wonton means "cloud," and in fact, these delicate shrimp

dumplings do float around like scattered clouds in the flavored cooking stock.

A little red vinegar added to the bowl provides excellent seasoning.

[wonton soup]

In a saucepan, slowly heat chicken stock, soy sauce, and sesame oil.
Drop bean sprouts into another saucepan of boiling water, cook for 1
minute, and drain. Bring 2 quarts water to a boil, add a little salt, then add
wontons, and cook for 2–3 minutes until they float to the top. Remove with
a slotted spoon and transfer to hot stock mixture. Simmer for 1 minute.
Transfer bean sprouts to a serving bowl, pour stock and wontons over
the top, and sprinkle with chopped green onion. Salt to taste and serve
very hot.

Serves 4
Prep and cooking time:
10 minutes

5 cups chicken stock
(see page 12)
1 tablespoon soy sauce
1 teaspoon sesame oil
1 cup bean sprouts
40 small wonton wrappers
(refrigerator section
of supermarket)
1 chopped green onion
Salt

[beef noodle soup]

Serves 6
Prep time: 20 minutes
Cooking time: 3 hours

2 pounds beef chuck roast
or steak
1 dried orange peel or
1 fresh orange
1 tablespoon cumin seeds
1 cinnamon stick
2 star anise
2 fresh red chile peppers
10 peppercorns
1/4 cup rice wine or sherry
1/4 cup soy sauce
8 ounces thin Chinese
egg noodles
Salt

Cut meat into 1-inch cubes and place in boiling water. Once water has returned to a boil, reduce heat and simmer for 10 minutes. Rinse under cold water.

If you use a fresh orange, rinse well, pat dry, and remove zest in a ribbon without removing the white part underneath. In a spice/tea ball (or cheesecloth that you tie into a pouch), combine cumin seeds, cinnamon stick, star anise, chile peppers, peppercorns, and the fresh (or dried) orange zest.

In a stockpot, combine meat, spice ball/pouch, rice wine, soy sauce, and 2 quarts cold water. Slowly bring to a boil, skim off any foam that surfaces, and season with a little salt. Then cover and simmer for about 2 1/2 hours until the meat is fall-apart tender.

Just before serving, place noodles in a large pot of boiling salted water, cook for 5 minutes, drain, and transfer to a serving bowl (preheated) or distribute in individual bowls. Skim off layer of fat that has formed on soup, pour soup over noodles, and serve.

You can also prepare this soup with chicken: Cook 1 whole chicken (2–3 pounds) in 2 quarts water with spices (except cumin), rice wine, and soy sauce for at least 1 hour. Drain chicken, remove skin and bones, slice meat, and return to stock after skimming off the fat. Finish as described above.

[shrimp and ginger soup]

Serves 2
Prep and cooking time:
20 minutes

3 green onions
1 small piece ginger
(½-inch section)
1 teaspoon oil
1 cube chicken bouillon
1–2 pinches crushed
red pepper flakes
½ pound live shrimp
(if available*)
1 teaspoon soy sauce
2 teaspoons sherry
Salt

Chop white part of green onions. Peel ginger and crush. In a saucepan, heat oil and sauté white part of onions and the ginger for 2 minutes.

Pour 2 cups water into the saucepan, bring to a boil, and add bouillon cube and crushed red pepper flakes. Add live shrimp and cook for 3 minutes. Pour contents of saucepan through a fine strainer placed over a bowl.

Peel shrimp and discard tails. Place heads (if you used live shrimp), shells, green onions, and ginger in a food processor and blend. Pour through the strainer over the bowl and press down using a rubber spatula to extract as much juice as possible.

Heat the strained liquid. Add soy sauce and sherry and season to taste (this forms the soup base). Transfer shrimp meat to individual bowls, pour soup base over the shrimp, and sprinkle with remaining green onions (cut into strips).

(*If live shrimp are unavailable, use uncooked shell-on shrimp.)

[bean sprout salad]

Serves 4
Prep and cooking time:
15 minutes

½ pound bean sprouts
2 slices cooked ham
1 small carrot
1 green onion or spring onion
1 clove garlic
2 tablespoons soy sauce
1 teaspoon cider vinegar
Several drops Tabasco
1 tablespoon peanut oil
1 teaspoon sesame oil
Salt

In a saucepan, boil some water. Rinse bean sprouts, add to boiling water, cook for 2 minutes, drain, rinse under cold water, and drain once again.

Trim any visible fat from ham and cut rest into strips. Peel carrot and grate into long threads. Rinse onion and chop the white part into the green part. Peel garlic and squeeze through a press. Mix garlic with soy sauce, cider vinegar, Tabasco, and peanut and sesame oils. Salt lightly. Add chopped green onion.

Place bean sprouts and carrot in a shallow bowl. Garnish with ham strips. Pour dressing over salad and serve chilled.

Variations: replace Tabasco with 1 small, finely chopped hot chile pepper. You can also replace the ham with poached or roasted chicken breast cut into strips.

For a more elegant meal, replace ham with fresh lump crabmeat (picked over to remove any bits of shell) and sprinkle salad with chopped chives. You can also vary the salad's flavor by adding cucumber cut into matchstick strips or thin strips of red or green bell pepper.

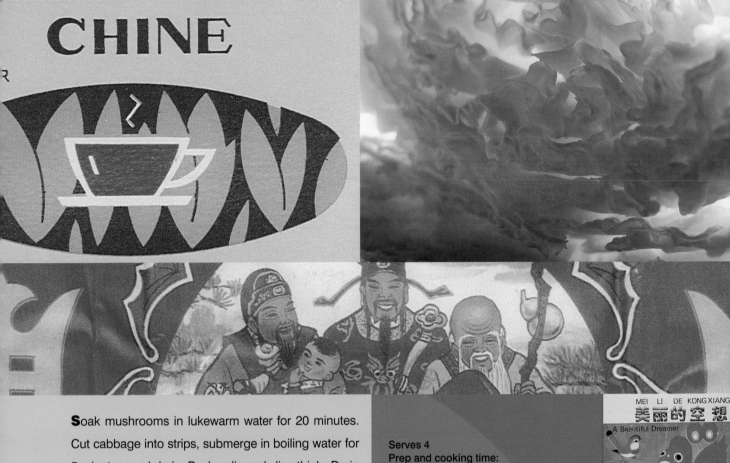

CHINE

Soak mushrooms in lukewarm water for 20 minutes. Cut cabbage into strips, submerge in boiling water for 5 minutes, and drain. Peel garlic and slice thinly. Drain mushrooms and save soaking liquid (strain). Remove/discard stems and cut caps into pieces.

Heat oil and sauté garlic slices until translucent. Add mushrooms, 2 tablespoons of the strained soaking liquid, and soy sauce. Salt lightly and cook for 2 minutes while stirring.

Add cabbage and Tabasco, stir, cover, and simmer over very low heat for 10 minutes. Salt more to taste.

Serves 4
Prep and cooking time:
15 minutes
Soaking time: 20 minutes

6 dried shiitake mushrooms
1 head Chinese (napa) cabbage
3 cloves garlic
2 tablespoons oil
2 tablespoons soy sauce
Several drops Tabasco
Salt

MEI LI DE KONG XIANG
美丽的空想
A Beautiful Dreamer

[chinese cabbage with mushrooms]

The Buddhist influence in China has been responsible for the birth of a delicious vegetarian cuisine full of rich flavors. Evoking neither suffering nor abstinence, this cooking style's vegetables are abundant, flavorful, and delicate—including tender white cabbage, crunchy bamboo shoots, mustard leaves, water chestnuts, and many different species of mushrooms.

[chicken and corn soup]

Serves 4
Prep and cooking time:
15 minutes

1 cup canned corn kernels
5 cups chicken stock
(see page 12)
⅓ pound boneless skinless
chicken breast
3 teaspoons cornstarch
1 teaspoon sesame oil
2 tablespoons rice wine
or sherry
½ teaspoon sugar
1 egg
1 chopped green onion
Salt and pepper

Rinse and drain corn; purée in a food processor. Heat stock, add puréed corn, season with salt and pepper, and simmer gently throughout the preparation of the rest of the soup.

Cut chicken breast into very small pieces, season with salt and pepper, and add to soup.

Stir cornstarch into 2 tablespoons cold water, add to soup, and stir for 1 minute. Then add sesame oil, rice wine (or sherry), and sugar; stir and simmer for 3 minutes.

Beat egg with a fork and pour into soup in a thin stream while stirring with chopsticks or a fork. Sprinkle with chopped green onion and serve.

[snow peas and water chestnuts]

Serves 4
Prep and cooking time:
20 minutes

⅓ pound snow peas
1 (8-ounce) can water
chestnuts, sliced
2 green onions or spring
onions
1 tablespoon canola oil
1 tablespoon soy sauce
1 teaspoon sugar
Pepper
1 teaspoon sesame oil

Remove ends and strings from snow peas, rinse, and cut diagonally into thirds. Rinse water chestnuts and drain. Peel outer layer from green onions and chop rest.

In a frying pan, heat oil and sauté green onions over high heat for 1 minute. Add snow peas, stir to coat evenly with oil, and sauté for 1 minute. Combine soy sauce, 3 tablespoons water, and sugar. Season with a little pepper.

Add soy sauce mixture to vegetables in frying pan and cook for 3 minutes while stirring constantly. Then add water chestnuts and cook for another 2 minutes to heat through. Drizzle with sesame oil, stir carefully, and serve while hot.

Serves 4
Prep time: 20 minutes
Soaking time: 20 minutes
Cooking time: 10 minutes

4 dried shiitake mushrooms
8 dried wood ear
mushrooms
½ cup sliced bamboo
shoots (canned)
¼ pound cooked roast pork
or 2 slices prosciutto
8 ounces tofu
2 eggs
5 cups chicken stock (see
page 12)
1 tablespoon sugar
3 tablespoons soy sauce
¼ teaspoon red chile paste
(Asian grocery or specialty
store)
¼ teaspoon ground white
pepper
3 tablespoons cider vinegar
Salt

[spicy peking soup]

Soak two types of mushroom separately in lukewarm water for 20 minutes. Rinse bamboo shoots and drain. Cut pork and tofu into slices of the same size. Beat eggs with a fork. Drain mushrooms, remove/discard stems, and slice caps.

Heat chicken stock. Add sugar, mushrooms, bamboo shoots, pork, and tofu; simmer for 5 minutes. Pour beaten eggs through a strainer into the soup while stirring the soup with chopsticks or a fork.

Remove from heat and add soy sauce, chile paste, white pepper, and cider vinegar. Season with salt and, if desired, more white pepper to taste. Stir carefully.

Additionally, you can add more or less chile paste as desired.

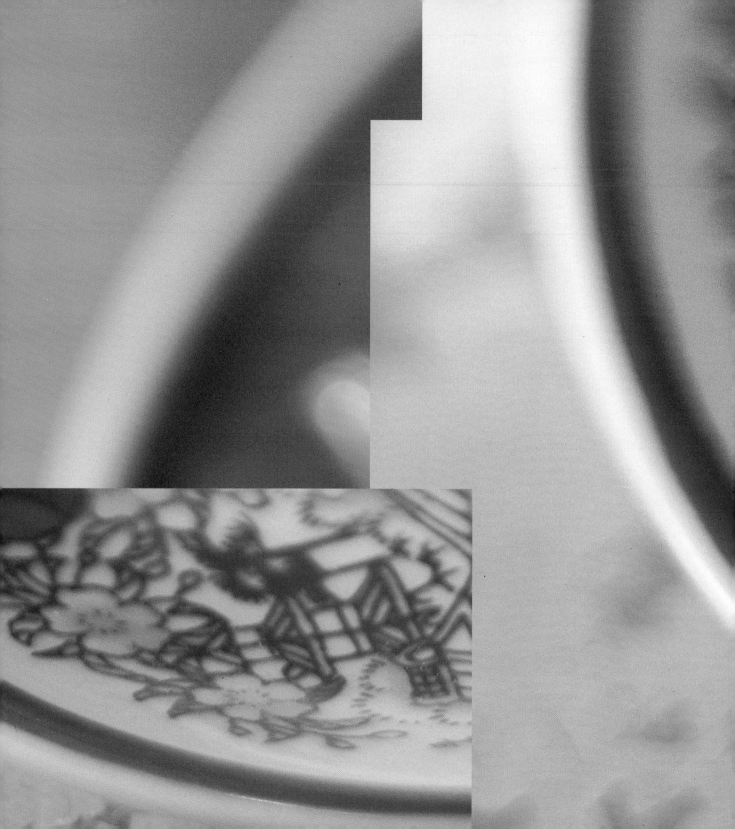

eggs, noodles, & rice

eggs, noodles, & rice

the staff of life

Rice and wheat are the foundations on which Chinese cuisine is built, with rice predominating in the south of China, and wheat in the north. But throughout China, people enjoy delicious dishes featuring the rice, soybean, and wheat noodles that Marco Polo brought back to the West—and now, we enjoy them, too. Nourishing and easy to prepare, Chinese noodles go with anything and adapt themselves to all styles, whether fried and crunchy, or in a soup. They take on the flavor of accompanying foods, making them universally popular.

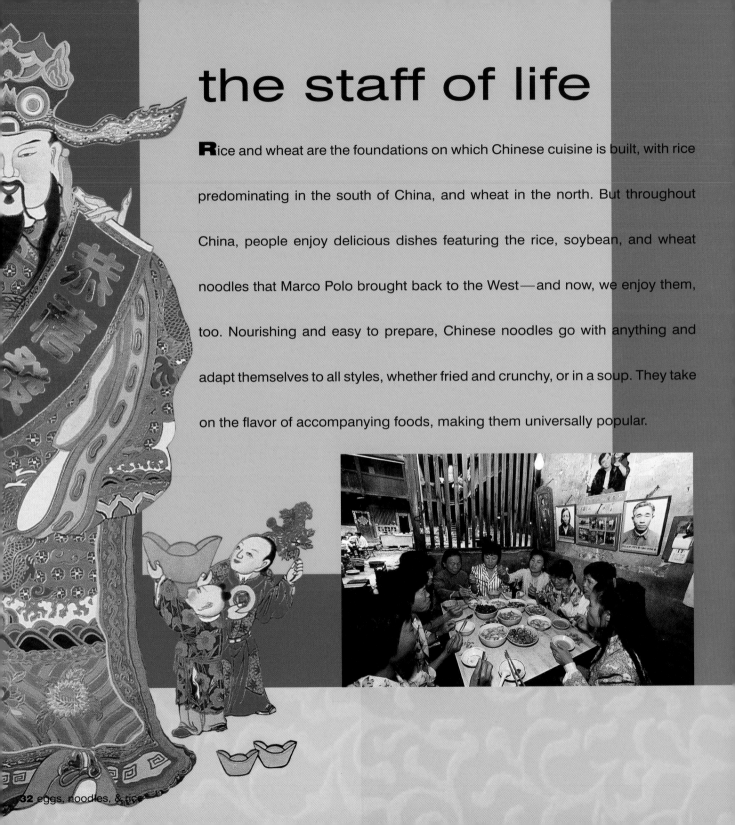

½ pound cooked roast pork
1 small can water chestnuts
(4 to 8 ounces; sliced)
1 small fresh chile pepper
2 green onions
2 cloves garlic
1 tablespoon lard or bacon
fat (or oil)
2 cups cooked rice,
prepared the day before
(see page 46)
2 tablespoons soy sauce

[fried rice with pork and water chestnuts]

Cut pork into strips. Rinse and drain water chestnuts. Remove seeds from chile pepper (wear gloves and don't touch your face), rinse green onions, and peel garlic; chop all three ingredients.

In a wok, melt lard and stir-fry garlic and green onion for 1 minute. Add chile pepper, stir-fry for 1 minute, then add rice and fry over high heat for 3–4 minutes.

Pour in soy sauce and stir. Add pork and water chestnuts and stir-fry for another 2 minutes to heat through.

[stir-fried noodles and vegetables]

Soak mushrooms in lukewarm water for 20 minutes. Rinse bamboo shoots. Peel carrot and cut into matchstick strips. Cut celery into matchstick strips. Remove ends and strings from snow peas, rinse, and cut diagonally into 3–4 pieces each. Rinse bell pepper, remove stem, seeds, and interior ribs; cut rest into strips and then into diamond shapes. Peel garlic and squeeze through a press. Rinse and slice green onions. Cut ginger into fine strips. Remove seeds from chile peppers and chop rest (wear gloves and don't touch your face).

In a small bowl, combine black bean sauce, soy sauce, sherry, 2 tablespoons water, sugar, and a little salt.

In a large saucepan, bring salted water to a boil, add noodles, and cook for 3 minutes. Drain, rinse under cold water, and drain once again.

Drain mushrooms, remove/discard stems, and slice caps.

In a wok, heat peanut oil and stir-fry mushrooms, carrot, snow peas, bell pepper, garlic, green onions, chile peppers, and ginger over high heat for 30 seconds. Add bamboo shoots, celery, and cooked noodles. Stir, drizzle with contents of sauce bowl, and stir-fry for 3 minutes. Add a few drops sesame oil and serve.

Serves 4
Prep and cooking time: 35 minutes
Soaking time: 20 minutes

8 dried shiitake mushrooms
¼ cup canned bamboo shoots
1 small carrot
1 stalk celery
1 cup snow peas, ends and strings removed
1 red bell pepper
3 cloves garlic
3 green onions
2 slices ginger
1–2 fresh chile peppers, green or red
1 teaspoon black bean sauce
¼ cup soy sauce
¼ cup sherry or rice wine
2 pinches sugar
½ pound fresh Chinese egg noodles (Asian grocery)
3 tablespoons peanut oil
½ tablespoon sesame oil
Salt

[chow mein]

Bring a large saucepan of water to a boil, salt lightly, and add noodles. Once water has returned to a boil, cook for 5 minutes.

Drain, drizzle with sesame oil, and stir carefully. Cut chicken breast and ham into bite-size strips; set aside. Rinse and peel all vegetables and ginger, and on a clean cutting board, cut into uniform strips.

Heat a sauté pan or wok. Add half the peanut oil and when it's very hot, sear chicken strips for 2 minutes while stirring constantly. Remove with a slotted spoon.

Wipe out the pan and heat remaining oil. Stir-fry vegetables and ginger over high heat for 2 minutes. Add ham, cooked chicken, and cooked noodles; stir-fry for 1 minute to heat through.

Combine stock, soy sauce, sherry, sugar, salt, and pepper; pour into the pan and stir until the mixture is hot. Drizzle with oyster sauce and serve immediately.

Serves 4
Prep and cooking time: 30 minutes

1/2 pound thin dried egg noodles
1 tablespoon sesame oil
1 chicken breast
2 slices cooked ham
1 red bell pepper
1 small carrot
1 stalk celery
1/4 cup canned bamboo shoots
6 fresh shiitake mushrooms
1/2 cucumber
2 slices fresh ginger
2 tablespoons peanut oil
1/2 cup chicken stock (see page 12)
1 tablespoon soy sauce
1 tablespoon sherry or rice wine
1/2 teaspoon sugar
1 tablespoon oyster sauce
Salt and pepper

[cellophane noodles with pork and tomato]

Serves 4
Prep and cooking time:
25 minutes
Marinating time: 15 minutes
Soaking time: 15 minutes

1/2 pound pork tenderloin
1 teaspoon potato starch
or cornstarch
1 tablespoon soy sauce
2 pinches sugar
1–2 pinches chili powder
5 ounces cellophane (mung
bean thread) noodles
2 large tomatoes
2 cloves garlic
2 green onions
3 tablespoons oil
2 1/4 cups chicken stock (see
page 12)
Salt

Slice pork very thinly and then into bite-size pieces. Mix potato starch with soy sauce, sugar, chili powder, and a little salt. Add pork slices, stir well to coat, and marinate for 15 minutes.

Soak noodles in lukewarm water for 15 minutes. Submerge tomatoes in boiling water for 30 seconds, rinse under cold water, peel, remove seeds, and chop rest. Peel garlic and green onions and mince both.

In a wok, heat oil and stir-fry garlic and green onions for 1 minute until translucent. Add pork and stir-fry for 2 minutes.

Drain noodles. Add to wok, stir, and add stock and chopped tomatoes. Bring to a boil, reduce heat, and simmer for several minutes until almost all the liquid has evaporated. Salt to taste and serve.

[crab egg foo yung]

Serves 2
Prep and cooking time:
15 minutes
Refrigeration time:
10 minutes

1/3 pound lump crabmeat
1/2 carrot cut into
matchstick strips
1 teaspoon cornstarch
4 eggs + 1 egg white
1/2 teaspoon sugar
1 tablespoon sherry or
rice wine
1 tablespoon soy sauce
1 1/2 tablespoons oil
1 chopped green onion
Salt and pepper

Combine crabmeat (checked over for shells and cartilage bits), carrot, salt, pepper, cornstarch, and egg white; refrigerate for 10 minutes.

Beat whole eggs together with sugar, sherry, soy sauce, 1 1/2 tablespoons water, salt, and pepper.

In a frying pan, heat 1/2 tablespoon of the oil and sauté crabmeat mixture for 2 minutes, then remove from pan. Wipe out pan and heat remaining oil. Pour in eggs and stir gently for 1 minute. Add crabmeat mixture and cook while stirring occasionally until the eggs have set.

Sprinkle with chopped green onion and serve.

[vegetable egg foo yung]

Soak mushrooms in lukewarm water for 30 minutes. Rinse half bell pepper and dice finely (minus seeds). Rinse bean sprouts. Peel and chop onion. Rinse and chop green part of green onion. Break eggs into a large bowl and whisk. Add stock, sherry, soy sauce, sugar, sesame oil, salt, and pepper; whisk to combine.

Rinse and drain mushrooms and cut into small pieces. In a large frying pan, heat half the peanut oil and stir-fry mushrooms, bell pepper, bean sprouts, and onion over high heat for 2 minutes. Remove and set aside.

Wipe out the pan. Heat remaining oil and pour in eggs. Cook for 1 minute while stirring. Then return stir-fried vegetables to the pan, plus the peas, and cook while stirring occasionally until the eggs have set. Sprinkle with onion greens and serve.

Serves 4
Soaking time: 30 minutes
Prep and cooking time:
20 minutes

3 dried wood ear mushrooms
½ red bell pepper
¼ cup canned or fresh bean
sprouts
1 small onion
Greens from 1 green onion
8 eggs
¼ cup vegetable stock
1 tablespoon sherry or rice wine
1 tablespoon soy sauce
1 teaspoon sugar
1 tablespoon sesame oil
2 tablespoons peanut oil
2 tablespoons frozen peas,
thawed
Salt and pepper

[marbled eggs]

Makes 8 eggs
Prep time: 10 minutes
Cooking time: 20 minutes

3 tablespoons loose-leaf black tea
1 tablespoon five-spice powder (see page 103)
1 tablespoon salt
8 eggs

Bring 5 cups water to a boil. Add tea leaves, five-spice powder, and salt; simmer for 10 minutes, covered.

In another large saucepan, cover eggs with cold water, bring to a boil, and cook for 5 minutes. Drain and then soak in cold water for 5 minutes. Drain again and tap them one by one to crack the shell on all sides but do not remove shell. Carefully submerge eggs into the boiling tea mixture and simmer over low heat for 10 minutes. Let cool in the liquid.

Peel eggs just before serving. Serve alone or as an appetizer.

[cellophane noodles with bean sprouts]

Serves 4
Prep time: 15 minutes
Soaking time: 20 minutes
Cooking time: 15 minutes

4 ounces cellophane (mung bean thread) noodles
½ pound fresh bean sprouts
8 green onions
2 cloves garlic
3 tablespoons oil
½ cup vegetable stock
1 tablespoon soy sauce
Several drops Tabasco
Salt and pepper

Soak noodles in a bowl of hot water for 20 minutes. Rinse bean sprouts under cold water. Rinse green onions and cut both white and green parts into pieces 1½ inches long. Peel and chop garlic.

Carefully drain noodles and using scissors, cut into pieces about 3 inches long.

In a wok, heat oil and stir-fry bean sprouts, green onions, and garlic for 3 minutes. Reduce heat and add cellophane noodles, vegetable stock, soy sauce, Tabasco, salt, and pepper. Stir and simmer over very low heat for 8–10 minutes and serve.

[noodles with beef and oyster sauce]

Serves 4–6
Prep and cooking time:
25 minutes

½ pound beef tenderloin
3 shallots
1½-inch section fresh ginger
¾ pound broccoli
1 small fresh red chile pepper
¼ cup oyster sauce
1 tablespoon soy sauce
1 tablespoon sherry or rice wine
1 teaspoon potato starch or cornstarch
1 pound flat rice noodles
1 tablespoon sesame oil
3 tablespoons peanut oil
1 cup chicken stock (see page 12)
Salt and pepper

Slice tenderloin crosswise (against the grain) and then cut into bite-size strips. Peel shallots and ginger and chop. Separate broccoli into small florets. Remove seeds from chile pepper and chop rest. Combine 2 tablespoons of the oyster sauce, soy sauce, sherry, and potato starch; set aside.

Cook noodles in boiling water for 3 minutes, rinse under cold water, and then add sesame oil.

In a wok, heat peanut oil, sear beef strips for 1 minute and remove. Then add broccoli, shallots, ginger, and chile pepper to wok; stir-fry for 1 minute and season with salt. Add sauce mixture and noodles and stir.

Return cooked meat to wok. Pour in stock, season with pepper, and let thicken while stirring. Drizzle with remaining oyster sauce and serve immediately.

Rice noodles are a translucent white color and are enjoyed in the Canton region and in Southeast Asia—especially Vietnam, where they are known for enhancing soup. They are light, delicate, and cook quickly.

[rice noodles with seafood]

Soak rice noodles in hot water for 25 minutes. Soak mushrooms in lukewarm water for 20 minutes.

In the meantime, cut squid into 1-inch pieces. Separate broccoli into very small florets. Cut ham into matchstick strips. Peel garlic and squeeze through a press. Peel then finely chop ginger. Remove seeds from chile peppers and chop rest finely (wear gloves and don't touch your face). Rinse then chop white and green parts of green onions separately.

Drain noodles. Drain mushrooms, rinse, remove/discard stems, and slice caps.

In a wok, heat oil and stir-fry garlic, ginger, and chile peppers for 30 seconds. Add mushrooms, broccoli, white part of green onions, and squid; stir-fry for 2 minutes. Then add noodles, ham, and shrimp. Sprinkle with sugar, salt, and pepper. Pour on stock, soy sauce, and sherry. Stir and cook over high heat for 3 minutes, making sure shrimp is cooked through. Transfer to a serving dish, sprinkle with green part of green onions, and serve hot.

Serves 4
Prep and cooking time:
45 minutes
Soaking time: 25 minutes

1/2 pound dried rice noodles
3 dried wood ear mushrooms
1/2 pound small cleaned squid
1/3 pound broccoli
1 slice cooked ham
3 cloves garlic
One piece ginger (3/4-inch section)
1–2 small green or red chile peppers
2 green onions
2 tablespoons oil
1/4 pound peeled shrimp
1 tablespoon sugar
1 cup chicken stock (see page 12)
3 tablespoons soy sauce
2 tablespoons sherry or rice wine
Salt and pepper

[fried rice]

Serves 6
Prep and cooking time:
30 minutes

2 cups rice
3 Chinese sausages
2 chicken breasts
2 tablespoons oyster sauce
¼ cup soy sauce
1 teaspoon cornstarch
2 drops sesame oil
3 tablespoons peanut oil
2 slices ham
3 green onions
2 eggs
¼ pound peeled *cooked* shrimp
Salt and pepper

Cook rice in a large saucepan of boiling salted water for 18 minutes. Cook sausages in boiling water for 10 minutes.

Finely slice chicken breasts and cut into bite-size strips. Combine oyster sauce, 2 tablespoons of the soy sauce, and cornstarch; then add 2 drops sesame oil and 1 tablespoon of the peanut oil. Marinate chicken slices in this mixture.

Cut ham into strips. Rinse and chop green onions. Beat eggs with a fork, cook in a nonstick pan, let cool, and cut into strips. Drain sausages and slice. Drain rice.

In a wok, heat remaining peanut oil. Drain chicken pieces but save the marinade, and stir-fry chicken along with green onions over high heat for 2 minutes. Add ham, sausage, shrimp, chicken marinade, remaining soy sauce, and then rice. Season with pepper. Stir-fry for 1–2 minutes until heated through. Sprinkle with egg strips and serve. You can also use leftover rice for this dish.

[vegetable fried rice]

This dish is prepared using day-old rice. Rice preparation: In a saucepan with a heavy base, combine rice, 2¼ cups water, and salt. Bring to a boil over high heat, cover with a tight-sealing lid, and simmer over very low heat for 20 minutes. Rice should be tender, still have a bite to it, yet not be mushy. It if tastes too starchy, add more water and cook longer. When finished, spread out rice on a large platter, let cool, and then refrigerate in a container.

The next day, soak mushrooms in a little lukewarm water for 20 minutes. Take rice out of refrigerator.

Rinse and drain bamboo shoots. Remove ends from green beans and cut rest diagonally into small pieces. Peel carrot and cut diagonally into thin slices. Rinse white parts of leeks very well and slice diagonally. Slice celery diagonally. Peel and chop garlic. Rinse and slice green onion. Remove seeds from chile pepper (if using; make sure to wear gloves and don't touch your face) and cut into fine rings.

Drain mushrooms and save the soaking liquid (strain). Remove/discard stems and slice caps. In a wok, heat oil and stir-fry garlic for 20 seconds. Then add mushrooms, green beans, carrot, leek, celery, chile pepper, and peas; stir-fry for 5 minutes.

Add bamboo shoots, stir, and then add rice; stir-fry over high heat for 3–4 minutes. Add green onion. Combine mushroom soaking liquid, salt, pepper, and the soy sauce. Pour over rice, stir, and make sure everything is heated through. Serve while hot.

Serves 4–6
Prep and cooking time:
55 minutes
Refrigeration time: 8 hours

1⅓ cups medium- or
short-grain rice
8 dried wood ear
mushrooms
¼ cup canned
bamboo shoots
¼ pound green beans
1 carrot
White part of 2 leeks
2 stalks celery
2 cloves garlic
1 green onion
1 hot fresh chile
pepper (optional)
3 tablespoons oil
⅓ cup frozen peas
2 tablespoons soy sauce
Salt and pepper

[spicy sichuan noodles]

Slice pork thinly against the grain and then cut into bite-size pieces; marinate with 1 tablespoon of the soy sauce, rice wine, salt, and pepper for 15 minutes. Peel ginger, garlic, and shallots; chop finely.

Cook noodles in boiling water for 3 minutes. Drain, rinse under cold water, place in a bowl, add sesame oil, stir, and cover.

In a wok, heat peanut oil and stir-fry garlic, ginger, and shallots for 30 seconds. Add pork and continue stirring until meat changes color. Then add remaining soy sauce, chicken stock, several drops Tabasco, and salt; continue cooking for 2 minutes.

Add noodles and cook to heat through for 1-2 minutes. Pour everything into a serving dish and grind some Sichuan peppercorns directly over the top.

Serves 4–5
Prep and cooking time:
25 minutes
Marinating time: 15 minutes

½ pound pork tenderloin
3 tablespoons soy sauce
1 tablespoon rice wine
or sherry
1 piece ginger
(1½-inch section)
6 cloves garlic
2 shallots
1 pound thin egg noodles,
fresh (Asian grocery)
1 tablespoon sesame oil
2 tablespoons peanut oil
1 cup chicken stock (see
page 12)
Several drops Tabasco
Sichuan peppercorns
Salt and pepper

[cantonese rice]

Cut ham into strips or cubes. Rinse then chop white part of green onion. Beat together eggs, sesame oil, and 1 pinch salt. Cook egg mixture in a small, nonstick frying pan and then dice.

Fluff cooked rice with a fork. In a wok, heat peanut oil and stir-fry rice for 5 minutes to heat thoroughly. Add ham pieces, peas, shrimp, and white part of green onion. Season with salt and pepper. Stir-fry over high heat for 3 more minutes, making sure shrimp is cooked through.

Add diced egg, stir, heat through, and serve.

Serves 4
Prep and cooking time:
20 minutes

1 small slice cooked ham
White part of 1 green onion
2 eggs
1 teaspoon sesame oil
3 cups cooked long-grain
rice, day-old (see method
on page 46)
2 tablespoons peanut oil
3 tablespoons cooked peas
3 tablespoons small
peeled shrimp
Salt and pepper

Serves 4
Prep time: 15 minutes
Cooking time: 5 minutes

½ pound thin egg noodles,
fresh (Asian grocery)
1 tablespoon sesame oil
½ cucumber
¼ pound fresh bean sprouts
4 cloves garlic
2 slices ginger
2 tablespoons soy sauce
2 tablespoons cider vinegar
2 teaspoons sugar
2 tablespoons tahini
(sesame paste)
1 tablespoon peanut oil
1 tablespoon Tabasco
Salt and pepper

[noodle salad
with sesame]

In a saucepan, bring water to a boil and salt lightly. Add noodles and once water has returned to a boil, cook for 3 minutes. Drain, rinse under cold water, drain again, and pour into a large bowl. Drizzle with sesame oil and stir.

Rinse cucumber and halve lengthwise, scrape out the seeds, and cut rest into fine strips. Rinse bean sprouts under cold water and drain. Peel garlic and squeeze through a press. Peel ginger, cut into pieces, and squeeze through a garlic press.

Combine soy sauce, cider vinegar, sugar, tahini, peanut oil, Tabasco, and the garlic and ginger. Season with salt and pepper and mix together vigorously.

Just before serving, stir cucumber and bean sprouts into noodles. Drizzle with dressing and toss.

steamed

precious
mouthfuls

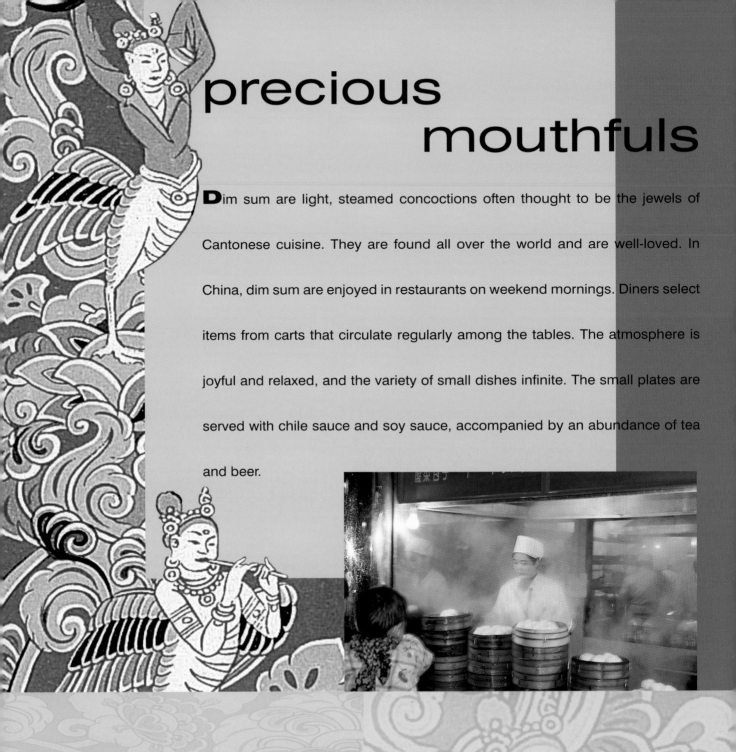

Dim sum are light, steamed concoctions often thought to be the jewels of Cantonese cuisine. They are found all over the world and are well-loved. In China, dim sum are enjoyed in restaurants on weekend mornings. Diners select items from carts that circulate regularly among the tables. The atmosphere is joyful and relaxed, and the variety of small dishes infinite. The small plates are served with chile sauce and soy sauce, accompanied by an abundance of tea and beer.

[cucumber stuffed with tofu]

Serves 4
Prep time: 15 minutes
Cooking time: 10 minutes

1 large cucumber
10–11 ounces fresh tofu
1 clove garlic
1 green onion
1 tablespoon cornstarch
2 pinches cayenne
1 tablespoon fresh
lemon juice
Salt and pepper

Peel cucumber (if desired) and cut off ends. Halve lengthwise, scrape out seeds, and cut rest into 1½-inch lengths.

Crumble tofu. Peel and crush garlic. Rinse and finely chop green onion. Mix these ingredients together with cornstarch, cayenne, fresh lemon juice, salt, and pepper. Add a little more salt, to taste—you'll be using this topping for the cucumber slices (which are mild) so it's fine if it is a little on the salty side.

Stuff cucumber pieces with this mixture. Arrange them side by side in the perforated basket of a steamer and place basket over a pan with ¾ inch of boiling water in the bottom. Cover and steam for 10 minutes.

Serve very hot.

[pork and shrimp dumplings]

Cut cabbage into fine strips, submerge in boiling water for 1 minute, and rinse under cold water.

Chop pork and shrimp together. Peel and grate carrot. Peel outer layer of green onion and chop white part finely. Peel and grate ginger.

In a bowl, combine pork and shrimp, carrot, green onion, ginger, five-spice powder, soy sauce, sugar, and cornstarch. Season with salt and pepper and mix thoroughly.

Using scissors, cut rice paper wrappers in half. Cover the work surface with a damp cloth. Place one half wrapper on the cloth and soften it by moistening it with a clean wet sponge (you can also dip it in a bowl of warm water). Round the two corners slightly with scissors. Place 1 heaping tablespoon of filling in the center. Bring the edges toward the center and pinch together firmly, then twist to seal in the filling. Follow this procedure to prepare all the dumplings.

Grease the bottom of the perforated basket of a steamer. Arrange dumplings in the basket so they do not touch. Place basket on top of a pan of simmering water, cover, and steam for 15 minutes. If the basket is too small to hold all the dumplings, steam in two batches.

Serve while hot with hoisin sauce.

Makes 16 dumplings
Prep time: 40 minutes
Cooking time: 15–30 minutes

⅓ pound Chinese (napa) cabbage
½ pound pork tenderloin
¼ pound peeled *cooked* shrimp
1 small carrot
1 green onion or spring onion
1 piece fresh ginger (¾-inch section)
2 pinches five-spice powder (see page 103)
1 teaspoon soy sauce
½ teaspoon sugar
1 tablespoon cornstarch
8 dried, round rice paper wrappers
Salt and pepper

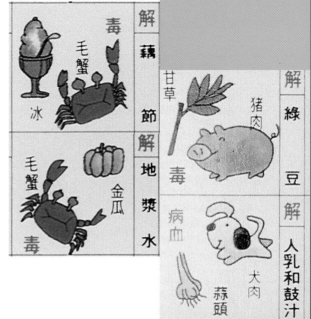

[steamed pork spareribs]

Serves 4
Prep time: 25 minutes
Cooking time: 1 hour
Standing time: 20 minutes

2 pounds pork spareribs cut into pieces
3 tablespoons fermented black beans (Asian grocery)
1 piece fresh ginger (1½-inch section)
4 cloves garlic
1–2 chile peppers
1 tablespoon potato starch or cornstarch
½ cup chicken stock (see page 12)
2 tablespoons rice wine or sherry
2 teaspoons sugar
2 tablespoons soy sauce
Salt and pepper

Rub spareribs with salt (sea salt or kosher salt if possible) and let stand for 20 minutes. Soak black beans in a bowl of cold water for 10 minutes. **P**reheat oven to 350°F.

Peel ginger and garlic and chop. Rinse chile peppers and chop. In a large baking dish, stir potato starch into stock. Add rice wine, sugar, soy sauce, ginger, garlic, chopped chile peppers, and pepper.

In a pan, boil some water, add pork, and simmer for 10 minutes. Drain beans and add to baking dish. Drain meat well, add to baking dish, and turn meat carefully to coat thoroughly with the other ingredients.

You're going to convert your oven broiling pan into a steaming apparatus. Place boiling water in the bottom. Put top of the broiler pan over it, and place your baking dish on top. Cover all the way over the top of the broiler pan with foil, giving the baking pan underneath some room to steam. Steam for one hour in the oven or until meat is fork tender. Skim any visible fat off the surface before serving.

Serves 4
Prep time: 15 minutes
Cooking time: 12–15 minutes

2 shallots
1 pound ground beef
2 egg whites
3 tablespoons chopped cilantro
1 tablespoon soy sauce
1 teaspoon sugar
1 tablespoon oil
2 pinches chili powder
2–3 cabbage leaves
Salt and pepper

[steamed beef meatballs]

Peel shallots and chop, then blend in a food processor. Add ground meat, egg whites, and $1/3$ cup water. Process for several seconds, then add cilantro, soy sauce, sugar, oil, chili powder, salt, and pepper.

Combine mixture and form into 12 meatballs. Use cabbage leaves to line the perforated basket of a steamer— put this over a pan containing 1 inch of simmering water. Place meatballs on cabbage leaves, reduce heat, cover, and steam for 12–15 minutes.

Transfer meatballs to a serving dish and serve immediately.

Serves 4
Prep time: 10 minutes
Cooking time: 20 minutes

2 eggs
$1/4$ cup sugar
$1/3$ cup milk
$3/4$ cup + 2 tablespoons rice flour
1 teaspoon baking powder
$1/8$ teaspoon pure vanilla
1 small pinch salt
1 teaspoon vegetable shortening
1 tablespoon butter
3 tablespoons honey or jam

[sponge cake]

Beat eggs with sugar. Add milk, rice flour, baking powder, vanilla, and salt. Mix carefully. Melt shortening and add to batter.

Grease an 8-inch cake pan and pour in batter. Cover with a sheet of aluminum foil or baking parchment and secure it with kitchen string. Place pan inside the perforated basket of a steamer over a pan containing 1 inch of simmering water. Cover, reduce heat, and steam for 20 minutes. (If cake pan doesn't fit in your stovetop steamer, use the broiler pan steamer method in the oven, described on page 56.)

Remove cake from pan while still hot. Serve hot or cold, with butter, and covered with melted honey or jam.

[side sauce]

Peel garlic and squeeze through a press. Finely chop chile pepper (if using). Dissolve sugar in vinegar and fish sauce. Add garlic, chile pepper, and ¼ cup water and stir.

This sauce goes well with steamed meatballs and wontons.

You can also prepare a variation with ginger: Combine 3 tablespoons fish sauce and 2 tablespoons fresh lime juice with 1 slice ginger (peeled and crushed) and 1 clove garlic (peeled and crushed).

Makes about ¾ cup
Prep and cooking time:
5 minutes

2 cloves garlic
½ chile pepper (optional)
1 tablespoon sugar
2 tablespoons vinegar
¼ cup fish sauce
(Asian grocery)

Serves 4
Prep time: 20 minutes
Cooking time: 15 minutes

1 long zucchini
4 small baby carrots
2 turnips
1 red bell pepper
½ pound broccoli
1 teaspoon green
peppercorns
1 teaspoon peanut oil
2 tablespoons soy sauce
1 teaspoon sesame oil
Salt

[steamed vegetables]

Rinse, peel, and cut the following into matchstick strips: zucchini, carrots, and turnips. Rinse bell pepper and cut into small diamonds. Separate broccoli into small florets.

Place vegetables in the perforated basket of a steamer. Place basket on top of a pan containing 1 inch of simmering water. Reduce heat, cover, and steam for 15 minutes. Transfer cooked vegetables to a serving dish and season with salt. Heat peanut oil in a small pan and add green peppercorns. Remove peppercorns with a slotted spoon and sprinkle oil over vegetables.

Drizzle with a mixture of soy sauce and sesame oil; serve while hot.

You can also prepare this dish with another type of fish, such as a carefully scaled bass or a sole that has been scraped but not skinned. This recipe is intended for pomfret, an Asian fish with a delicate meat resembling John Dory.

[whole sea bream with ginger]

Serves 4
Prep time: 15 minutes
Cooking time: 30 minutes

1 sea bream (about 2 pounds), cleaned and scaled (ask your fishmonger)
2 green onions
1 clove garlic
1 piece fresh ginger (1½-inch section)
1 tablespoon oil
1 tablespoon soy sauce
1 tablespoon white vermouth
1 tablespoon Chinese fermented black bean sauce
½ teaspoon sugar
Salt and pepper

Carefully rinse sea bream and check for scales. Wipe with paper towels, inside and out. Season interior with salt and pepper. Score sides of fish at regular intervals, season with salt and pepper, and rub it in so the seasonings penetrate. Place fish in a long dish inside the perforated basket of a steamer. (If fish doesn't fit in your stovetop steamer basket, use the broiler pan steamer method in the oven, described on page 56. Also, you can set the fish on top of a sushi mat set on the broiler pan.)

Rinse green onions, peel garlic, and chop both. Peel ginger and cut into fine strips. Combine green onions, garlic, and ginger with oil, soy sauce, vermouth, black bean sauce, and sugar. Pour over fish and also into the inside cavity.

Place steamer dish on top of a pan containing 1 inch of boiling water (or use oven-steaming method). Reduce heat so the water boils gently, cover, and steam for 25–30 minutes. Serve hot in the dish in which it was cooked.

[pork wontons]

Soak mushrooms in lukewarm water for 20 minutes. Chop pork. Rinse water chestnuts and chop coarsely. Rinse green onions, peel away outer layer and any wilted parts, and chop rest finely. Beat egg. Drain mushrooms, remove/discard stems, and chop caps coarsely.

Mix together pork, mushrooms, water chestnuts, green onions, egg, cornstarch, sugar, ½ teaspoon of the sesame oil, peanut oil, cayenne, salt, and pepper.

Place a little filling on each wonton skin near the side closest to you. Moisten the edges, then fold edges over filling and pinch together firmly on all sides to seal in the filling (see photo at right).

Grease the bottom of the perforated basket of a steamer. Arrange wontons inside so they do not touch. Brush tops with remaining sesame oil. Place basket on top of a pan containing simmering water, cover, and steam for 15 minutes. If the basket is too small to hold all the wontons, steam in two batches.

Serves 4–5
Prep time: 40 minutes
Cooking time: 15 minutes
Soaking time: 20 minutes

3 dried wood ear
mushrooms
½ pound pork tenderloin
¼ cup canned sliced
water chestnuts
2 green onions
1 egg
1 tablespoon cornstarch
½ teaspoon sugar
1 tablespoon sesame oil
½ tablespoon peanut oil
⅛ teaspoon cayenne
powder
20 wonton wrappers
(refrigerator section)
Vegetable oil
Salt and pepper

[braised zucchini]

Rinse zucchini, pat dry, cut into quarters lengthwise, and then into pieces 1½ inches long. Peel garlic and crush.

In a wok or frying pan, heat oil and stir-fry zucchini and garlic for 2 minutes (but don't let the garlic turn brown).

Combine soy sauce, sugar, and chicken stock. Add to zucchini pan and simmer uncovered over low heat for 2 minutes. Season with salt and pepper.

Pour pan contents into a baking dish. Place dish inside the perforated basket of a steamer and set over a pan containing 1 inch of boiling water.

Cover the steamer, reduce heat to very low, and let steam for 20 minutes. Serve while hot.

Serves 4
Prep time: 15 minutes
Cooking time: 25 minutes

1 pound small, long zucchini
2 cloves garlic
2 tablespoons oil
2 tablespoons soy sauce
1 teaspoon sugar
⅓ cup chicken stock
(see page 12)
Salt and pepper

[eight treasures rice pudding]

Serves 4–5
Prep time: 35 minutes
Cooking time: 1 hour

1 cup + 2 tablespoons
round-grain rice
1 tablespoon flour
7 ounces red bean paste (Asian
grocery)
1 tablespoon oil
8 dates
1 tablespoon raisins
5 maraschino cherries
2 sections candied orange peel
1 stick candied angelica*
(*optional, if available)
1 slice candied pineapple
2 tablespoons vegetable shortening
2 tablespoons sugar
1 tablespoon skinless, blanched almonds

For the syrup:
1/4 cup sugar
2 teaspoons cornstarch
Several drops almond extract

Rinse rice in cold water, cover with a generous amount of cold water in a pot, and bring to a boil. Cover and cook for 25 minutes. Combine flour and bean paste and begin to heat in a small frying pan. Add oil, mix well, and sauté paste over medium heat for 5 minutes while stirring constantly. Let cool.

Cut dates in half and remove pits. Rinse raisins. Cut maraschino cherries in half (remove pits if present). Cut candied orange peel into small cubes and angelica into fine strips. Cut pineapple into small triangles.

Grease a 4-cup (one quart) charlotte mold (or any small mold or Bundt pan) with a little of the vegetable shortening. Decorate the bottom and sides with candied fruits and almonds, placing all the cherry halves in the bottom of the pan in the center.

Drain rice and mix with remaining vegetable shortening and sugar. Place a layer of rice in the mold, pressing down gently to pack it. Then make a layer using all of the bean paste mixture and top this with the remaining rice. Press down again and smooth out the top. The rice must not come more than 1½ inches from the top of the mold.

Place mold in the perforated basket of a steamer on top of a pan containing 1½ inches boiling water. Cover (if the lid won't fit, use aluminum foil to cover the steamer), reduce heat so the water boils gently, and steam for 1 hour.

Prepare the syrup: Dissolve sugar in ⅔ cup water and bring to a boil. Stir cornstarch into 2 tablespoons water, pour into boiling sugar water, and cook for 2 minutes while stirring constantly. Add almond extract and remove from heat. Reverse the rice pudding from the mold onto a platter, pour hot syrup over the top, and serve.

[monkfish with lemon grass]

Serves 4
Prep time: 15 minutes
Cooking time: 30 minutes

1 onion
3 stalks fresh lemon grass
2 pounds monkfish fillets
1 heart of romaine lettuce
2 sprigs fresh mint
½ cucumber
1 carrot
3 ounces rice noodles
(vermicelli-sized)
Oil
Salt and white pepper

Peel and chop onion. Rinse lemon grass, remove/discard outer layer, and thinly slice rest. Rinse monkfish and cut into thick portions. Season each portion generously with salt and pepper.

Grease the perforated basket of a steamer. Place monkfish inside and sprinkle with chopped onion and lemon grass. Place basket on top of a pan containing about an inch of boiling water. Cover, reduce heat so the water boils gently, and steam for 30 minutes.

Rinse lettuce leaves well. Rinse mint and separate into smaller sprigs. Peel cucumber, halve and scrape out seeds, and then cut into sticks. Peel carrot and cut into sticks.

In a saucepan, bring water to a boil, add rice noodles, and cook for 5 minutes. Drain and rinse under cold water.

Five minutes before fish is done cooking, top with carrot sticks. Arrange lettuce, noodles, cucumber and mint sprigs around the edges of a serving dish. Place monkfish slices in the center and serve, topped with the steamed carrot sticks. (Discard lemon grass pieces before serving fish.)

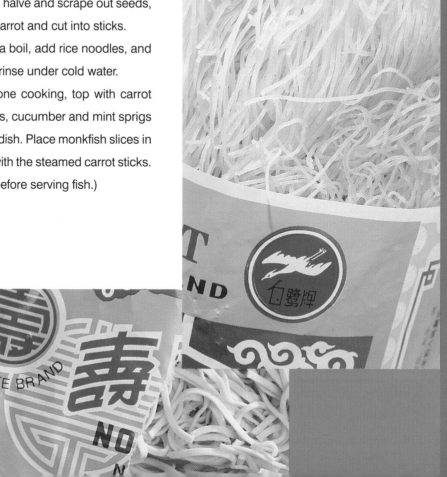

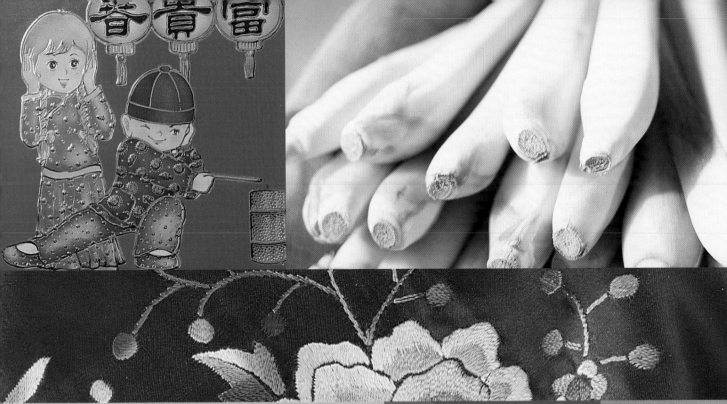

Soak two types of mushroom separately in lukewarm water for 20 minutes. Rinse green onions and slice finely. Cut chicken breasts into bite-size strips. Whisk potato starch into rice wine mixed with soy sauce.

Drain mushrooms, remove/discard stems, and slice caps. Place chicken, green onions, mushrooms, and oyster sauce in a heatproof dish, season with salt and pepper, and stir well.

Place dish inside the perforated basket of a steamer containing 1 inch of boiling water. Cover and steam for 15–20 minutes. (If your dish doesn't fit into your stovetop steamer, use oven-steamer method described on page 56.)

Serves 6
Prep time: 25 minutes
Cooking time: 15–20 minutes
Soaking time: 20 minutes

8 dried shiitake mushrooms
6 dried wood ear mushrooms
4 green onions
6 chicken breasts
(preferably free range)
1 tablespoon potato starch
or cornstarch
2 tablespoons rice wine
or sherry
1 tablespoon soy sauce
3 tablespoons oyster sauce
Salt and pepper

Mother Rabbit and the Tiger
MU TU HE LAO HU
母兔和老虎
新华出版社

[mushroom chicken]

Chinese cuisine uses lots of dried mushrooms, which are

not only esteemed for their flavor and texture but also for

their nutritional value, attributed to them by the Taoist

tradition. Wood ear mushrooms grow on trees and can be

found dried or fresh. Shiitakes are also available dried or

fresh. Fresh versions tend to be less pungent, and also

less aromatic, but either dried or fresh will work in the

recipes in this book.

[shrimp balls]

Serves 4–6
Prep time: 20 minutes
Standing time: 15 minutes
Cooking time: 8 minutes

Peel shallots. Chop shallots and water chestnuts, plus chicken breast and bacon.

In a food processor, process shrimp, shallots, water chestnuts, chicken, and bacon. Stir potato starch into rice wine and add to food processor along with egg white and sesame oil. Season with salt. Process again to obtain a smooth mixture. Refrigerate for 15 minutes.

Take teaspoons of the shrimp mixture and roll them into balls with your hands (works best if you grease your hands). Grease the perforated basket of a steamer and place the shrimp balls inside. Place on top of a pan containing 1 inch simmering water, cover, and steam for 8 minutes.

Rinse lettuce leaves and pat dry well. Arrange steamed shrimp balls on top of lettuce to serve.

2 shallots
¼ cup water chestnuts
¼ pound chicken breast
3 slices uncooked bacon
¾ pound peeled shrimp
1 tablespoon potato starch
or cornstarch
1 tablespoon rice wine
or sherry
1 egg white
1 teaspoon sesame oil
1 heart of romaine lettuce
Oil
Salt

[peanut buns]

Makes 8 buns
Prep time: 15 minutes
Cooking time: 15 minutes

In a heatproof dish, combine rice flour and potato starch. Make a well in the center and gradually add 1 cup boiling water while stirring. When you have a uniform dough, place dish in the perforated basket of a steamer containing 1 inch boiling water. Cover and steam for 15 minutes (use aluminum foil if cover doesn't fit).

Preheat the oven to 350°F. Then, in a food processor, process peanuts into a coarse powder and then add sugar; process to combine.

Let dough cool outside the steamer until lukewarm; separate into 8 portions. Shape each into a ball. Flatten into pancakes with a 3- to 4-inch diameter. Place sugared peanuts in the center of each, fold edges up around the filling and pinch together firmly to seal.

Arrange these buns on a parchment-lined baking sheet; dust with rice flour. Bake briefly (middle rack) until lightly golden.

¾ cup + 1 tablespoon
rice flour
¼ cup potato starch
or cornstarch
1 cup shelled,
unsalted peanuts
⅔ cup sugar
Rice flour for dusting

Serves 4
Prep time: 20 minutes
Cooking time: 15 minutes
Soaking time: 20 minutes
Marinating time: 15 minutes

3 dried wood ear
mushrooms
1 pound chicken breasts
2 cloves garlic
2 tablespoons oil
2 tablespoons soy sauce
1 tablespoon sugar
2 tablespoons rice wine
or sherry
2 small carrots
2 stalks celery
8 small broccoli florets
Salt and pepper

[sliced chicken
with vegetables]

Soak mushrooms in lukewarm water for 20 minutes. Slice chicken breasts. Peel garlic and squeeze through a press. Combine oil, 1 pinch salt, garlic, soy sauce, sugar, and rice wine. Pour over chicken slices, mix well, and marinate for 15 minutes.

Peel carrots and cut diagonally into thin slices. Rinse celery and slice. Drain mushrooms, remove/discard stems, and slice caps.

Transfer chicken and marinade to a heatproof dish. Add carrots, celery, mushrooms, and broccoli; stir. Cover dish with a sheet of aluminum foil and place inside the perforated basket of a steamer. Place basket on top of the bottom section containing boiling water. Cover the steamer (use more aluminum foil if steamer cover doesn't fit), reduce heat, and steam for 15 minutes. Serve in the dish in which it was cooked. (You can also use the oven-steamer method as described on page 56.)

fried

fried

hot and crisp

Chinese fried foods are a specialty of the south, where all sorts of small noodles, wontons, and potstickers are briefly dunked into a deep-fryer and then enjoyed with sweet sauces. These appetizers are part of the dim sum cuisine that is specific to Canton. Vietnamese imperial rolls are wrapped in rice paper, whereas their Chinese and Indonesian counterparts are surrounded by a wrapper made from flour.

[spicy shrimp fritters]

Serves 4
Prep time: 40 minutes
Marinating time: at least
1 hour

20 king prawns
2 cloves garlic
1 piece fresh ginger (1/2-inch section)
1 small red chile pepper
1/8 teaspoon nutmeg
1 tablespoon fresh lime juice
1/3 cup coconut milk
1 cup potato starch or cornstarch
Oil for frying
Hoisin sauce (optional)
Salt

Peel shrimp, leaving the tail attached. Slit down the back and remove black vein. Rinse and dry thoroughly.

Peel garlic and ginger and grate both finely. Remove seeds from chile pepper (wear gloves) and mince. Combine garlic, ginger, chile pepper, nutmeg, fresh lime juice, coconut milk, and a little salt. Add shrimp and turn to coat evenly. Marinate in the refrigerator for 1 hour.

Remove shrimp from marinade and drain. Pour potato starch onto a plate and dredge shrimp in it. In a wok, heat oil and fry shrimp in small batches for about 2 minutes until golden brown. (To test the oil, lower a wooden spoon handle down into it. When it's hot enough, lots of tiny bubbles will congregate around it.) Then drain on a paper towel-lined plate.

Serve with hoisin sauce if desired.

[imperial rolls]

Makes 6 rolls
Prep and cooking time:
1 hour
Soaking time: 20 minutes

5 dried wood ear
mushrooms
1 carrot
1/2 head Chinese (napa)
cabbage
1/2 pound pork tenderloin
1/3 pound peeled *uncooked*
shrimp
1 green onion
2 tablespoons soy sauce
2 tablespoons rice wine
or sherry
1/4 teaspoon cornstarch
3 cloves garlic
1 slice fresh ginger
6 rice paper wrappers
Beaten egg for sealing
wrappers
Oil for frying
Salt and pepper

Soak mushrooms in lukewarm water for 20 minutes. Peel and grate carrot. Rinse and cut cabbage into fine strips. Chop pork, shrimp, and green onion together and add 1 teaspoon of the soy sauce, 1 teaspoon of the rice wine, cornstarch, salt, and pepper.

Peel garlic and ginger and chop both finely. Drain mushrooms, remove/discard stems, and slice caps.

In a frying pan or wok, heat 1 tablespoon oil and stir-fry garlic and ginger for 10 seconds. Add mushrooms, carrot, cabbage strips, pork-shrimp mixture and remaining soy sauce and rice wine; stir-fry over high heat for 5 minutes. Drain mixture.

Submerge rice paper wrappers into a large bowl full of lukewarm water to soften them, one by one. Mound a little filling in a strip about 3 inches long and 3/4 inch from the edge nearest you. Fold edge nearest you over the filling, then fold in the sides and roll the wrapper closed, away from you. Brush the end with a little beaten egg and press together to seal the roll. Repeat until you have used all 6 wrappers.

Clean the wok or use a deep-fryer or pot and heat oil for frying, to 350–375°F (use an oil thermometer). Fry rolls in small batches until golden brown. Drain on paper towels and serve hot.

["stuffed" crab claws]

Crack crab claws, being careful to leave the pincers intact. Remove all meat and pull out cartilage. Separate 2 halves of each pincer, rinse and dry. Remove crust from bread, tear bread into pieces, place in a food processor, and process into large crumbs. Transfer to a small bowl.

Separate egg. Peel shallots and slice. Combine shallots, crabmeat, shrimp, and egg white in a food processor and process into a uniform mixture. Add soy sauce, rice wine, a little cayenne pepper to taste, salt, and pepper.

Beat egg yolk with a fork. Place breadcrumbs in a shallow bowl.

Moisten your hands and shape crab-shrimp mixture into 8 balls. Dip each ball in beaten egg, then roll in breadcrumbs and pierce each ball with one crab pincer so the end is exposed. Place on a platter so they do not touch. Refrigerate for 15 minutes.

In a wok, heat oil for frying. Brown crab claws by immersing in hot oil (should register 350–375°F; use an oil thermometer) for 2–3 minutes. Remove with a slotted spoon and drain on paper towels. Serve while hot with sweet and sour sauce (see page 90).

Makes 8 claws
Prep time: 40 minutes
Refrigeration time:
15 minutes
Cooking time: 10 minutes

4 fresh or frozen crab claws
2 slices white bread
1 egg
2 shallots
½ pound peeled *uncooked* shrimp
1 tablespoon soy sauce
1 tablespoon rice wine or sherry
⅛ teaspoon cayenne
3–4 tablespoons breadcrumbs
Oil for frying
Salt and pepper

7 ounces tofu
1 scant cup flour
1/2 teaspoon baking powder
1/8 teaspoon turmeric
1/4 teaspoon chili powder
1 egg
Oil for frying
Salt and pepper

[tofu fritters]

Submerge tofu in boiling water, leave for 5 minutes, drain, rinse under cold water, and then mash with a fork.

Combine flour, baking powder, turmeric, chili powder, salt, and pepper. Add egg, puréed tofu, and about 1/4 cup water to form a dough that is very soft but not runny (add more water or more flour as needed to achieve proper texture).

Heat oil for deep-frying to 350–375°F (use oil thermometer). Drop teaspoons full of dough into oil in small batches. Let brown for several minutes. Drain on paper towels and serve immediately.

[puffed shrimp chips]

Serves 3–4
Prep and cooking time:
15 minutes

1 large package shrimp
chips (Asian grocery)
1 quart oil for frying

In a large, deep-frying pan, heat oil for frying to 350–375°F (use oil thermometer). When the oil is ready, drop several chips in the oil (make sure they do not touch). As soon as they have puffed up, remove them with a slotted metal utensil, and drain on paper towels. Repeat to cook all shrimp chips.

Transfer to a serving dish lined with a white cloth and serve alongside an aperitif. Perhaps some plum wine?

[fried wontons]

Chop shrimp coarsely. Rinse and chop bamboo shoots. Finely chop green onion. Combine shrimp, ground pork, bamboo shoots, green onion, egg yolk, sugar, cornstarch, and sesame oil. Add a little salt and pepper, mix well, and refrigerate for 15 minutes.

Place 1 teaspoon filling in the center of each wonton wrapper. Moisten all the way around the edges of the wrapper with a little water. Fold 2 opposite corners over the filling and pinch together, then fold in the other 2 corners and pinch together firmly to seal.

In a wok or deep-fryer, heat oil for frying to 350–375°F (use an oil thermometer). Brown wontons in small batches in the oil. As soon as they are golden, remove with a slotted metal utensil, and drain on paper towels. Serve while hot with sweet and sour sauce (see page 90).

Serves 4–5
Prep and cooking time:
40 minutes
Standing time: 15 minutes

¼ pound peeled *uncooked* shrimp
¼ cup canned bamboo shoots
1 green onion
¼ pound *ground* pork tenderloin (ask your butcher)
1 egg yolk
½ teaspoon sugar
1 teaspoon cornstarch
Several drops sesame oil
20 wonton wrappers (refrigerated section)
Oil for frying
Salt and pepper

Makes 25 wontons
Prep and cooking time:
45 minutes

2/3 cup dates
1/4 cup walnut halves
1 orange
1 egg white
25 wonton wrappers
(refrigerated section)
Oil for frying
Powdered sugar

[sweet fried wontons]

Remove/discard pits from dates and chop rest. Coarsely chop walnuts. Rinse orange well and remove about 1/2 teaspoon of zest. Squeeze juice from half the orange. **C**ombine dates, walnuts, and zest; moisten with a little of the orange juice.

Place a diagonal strip of filling on a wonton wrapper, almost in the center, and fold one side of the wrapper over the filling. Moisten your index finger in beaten egg white and spread a little on the top of this flap. Tuck the pointed corner under the filling and roll up the wonton skin. Pinch together at both ends and twist, like a candy wrapper (as pictured).

In a wok, heat oil to 350–375°F (use an oil thermometer) and brown wontons in small batches in the oil for 2 minutes. Drain on a paper towel-lined plate and serve, hot or cold, sprinkled with powdered sugar.

These caramelized fritters have been made world-famous by Chinese restaurants. Be careful when you eat them—they're hot inside and the caramel sticks to your teeth! But, they're worth it…

[caramelized apple fritters]

Serves 4
Prep and cooking time:
30 minutes

1 scant cup flour
1 teaspoon baking powder
4 apples
1 egg white
1 cup + 2 tablespoons sugar
1 tablespoon sesame seeds
Oil for frying

Stir flour and baking powder into $1/2$ cup water (add a little more water if needed to form a batter for dipping the apples into). Peel apples, cut into quarters, and remove/discard cores. Beat egg white into soft peaks and carefully fold into batter.

Heat oil in a wok or pot to 350–375°F (use an oil thermometer). One by one, dip apple pieces in batter and then drop into hot oil. Fry in small quantities for 2 minutes, until golden. Drain on paper towels.

Just before serving, prepare a bowl of cold water with several ice cubes. Reheat oil and fry fritters for another 2 minutes and then drain. Dissolve sugar in $1/4$ cup water, add sesame seeds, and bring to a boil. When the sugar begins to caramelize, drop fritters into syrup one by one and turn to coat evenly. Transfer directly to ice water to harden caramel coating. Remove at once and serve immediately.

[lime chicken]

Remove skin from chicken breasts and cut chicken into bite-size pieces. Place on a plate. Peel and grate ginger; mix with rice wine, salt, and pepper. Brush this mixture onto chicken pieces and marinate for 30 minutes.

Prepare the sauce: Squeeze juice from 2–3 limes to obtain about ½ cup fresh lime juice. Peel garlic and ginger and squeeze both through a garlic press. In a small bowl, combine garlic, ginger, sugar, the 1 tablespoon potato starch, rice wine, and salt. Mix well. Bring stock to a boil in a pot, add sauce-ingredient mixture, stir, and remove from heat. Wait 1 minute and then add several drops sesame oil.

Place egg yolks in a small bowl and beat lightly with a fork. Spread the ¾ cup potato starch on a plate. Dip chicken pieces in egg yolk and then potato starch, turning to coat evenly.

In a wok or deep-fryer, heat oil for frying to 350–375°F (use oil thermometer) and fry chicken pieces in small batches until golden brown. As soon as they are done, drain on paper towels.

If desired, heat sauce over low heat while stirring. Cut one lime into wedges and arrange it around the chicken; serve very hot, with the sauce alongside for dipping or drizzling.

Serves 4
Prep and cooking time: 20 minutes
Marinating time: 30 minutes

1 pound chicken breast
1 piece fresh ginger (½-inch section)
2 tablespoons rice wine or sherry
2 egg yolks
¾ cup potato starch or cornstarch
Oil for frying
Salt and pepper

For the sauce:
3–4 limes
2 cloves garlic
1 piece fresh ginger (½-inch section)
2 tablespoons sugar
1 tablespoon potato starch or cornstarch
1 tablespoon rice wine or sherry
⅓ cup chicken stock (see page 12)
Yellow food coloring (optional)
Several drops sesame oil

[spring rolls]

Makes 6 rolls
Prep and cooking time: 1 hour
Marinating time: 10 minutes

3 dried wood ear mushrooms
¼ pound pork tenderloin
¼ pound chicken breast
1 tablespoon soy sauce
1 tablespoon rice wine or sherry
1 teaspoon sugar
4 drops sesame oil
1 teaspoon cornstarch
¼ pound ham
¼ cup bamboo shoots
½ pound bean sprouts
2 tablespoons peanut oil
6 rice paper wrappers
Oil for frying
Salt and pepper

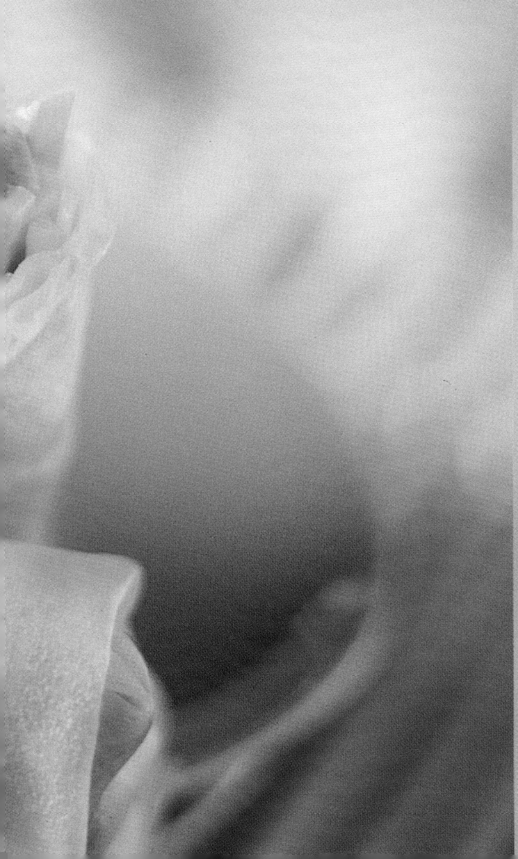

Soak mushrooms in lukewarm water for 20 minutes. Cut pork and chicken breast into bite-size pieces. Combine soy sauce, rice wine, sugar, sesame oil, cornstarch, salt, and pepper. Pour ⅓ of this mixture onto pork and chicken, stir well, and marinate for 10 minutes.

Cut ham and bamboo shoots into fine strips. Rinse bean sprouts. In a wok, heat 1 tablespoon of the peanut oil and stir-fry bean sprouts for 1 minute. Remove and wipe out wok. Drain mushrooms, remove/discard stems, and slice caps.

In the wok, heat remaining 1 tablespoon peanut oil and stir-fry pork and chicken for 2 minutes or until cooked through. Add mushrooms, bamboo shoots, ham, and the bean sprouts. Add remaining soy sauce mixture, and stir-fry over low heat for 3 minutes. Let cool.

Submerge rice paper wrappers in a bowl of lukewarm water to soften them, one by one. On each wrapper, mound a little filling in a strip about 3 inches long and ¾ inch from the edge nearest you. Fold edge closest to you over the filling, then fold in the sides and roll the wrapper closed, away from you. Prepare remaining rolls in the same way.

In a wok or deep-fryer, heat oil for frying 350–375°F (use oil thermometer) and brown spring rolls in small batches in the oil, then drain on a paper towel-lined plate. Serve with a side sauce (see page 58).

You can also serve spring rolls chilled, without frying (as shown at left).

[sweet and sour pork]

Serves 6
Prep and cooking time:
1 hour
Marinating time: 30 minutes

1 pound pork tenderloin
2 tablespoons rice wine
or sherry
2 tablespoons soy sauce
1 tablespoon sesame oil
1 carrot
½ green bell pepper
½ red bell pepper
2 stalks celery
1 onion
2 pineapple slices
2 eggs
¾ cup potato starch
or cornstarch
1 tablespoon oil
⅔ cup sweet and sour
sauce (see page 90)
Oil for frying
Salt

Cut pork into ¾-inch cubes. In a bowl, combine rice wine, soy sauce, sesame oil, and salt. Add pork, toss, and marinate in the refrigerator for 30 minutes.

In the meantime, peel carrot, slice lengthwise and then cut into ¾-inch lengths. Cook in boiling water for 3 minutes and drain. Cut bell peppers into ¾-inch squares. Slice celery. Peel onion and dice. Cut pineapple slices into small pieces.

Beat eggs lightly with a fork. Add 4 tablespoons of the potato starch and stir. In a deep-fryer, heat oil for frying to 350–375°F (use an oil thermometer).

Drain pork from the marinade, dust with some of the remaining potato starch, and dip in egg mixture, turning each piece to coat evenly.

Using a slotted metal utensil, place pork pieces in hot oil and fry in small batches for 5 minutes or until browned (and cooked through). As soon as they are done, drain on paper towels.

In a wok, heat 1 tablespoon oil and stir-fry carrot, bell peppers, celery, and onion over high heat for 3 minutes. Add sweet and sour sauce, fried pork pieces, and pineapple. Simmer for 3–4 minutes over medium heat and serve while hot.

Peel green onion and garlic and chop both finely. Peel and grate ginger.

Dissolve sugar over low heat in soy sauce, cider vinegar, rice wine, and 1/2 cup water.

Sauté green onion, garlic, and ginger in hot oil for 2 minutes. Add sugar-soy mixture and tomato paste, then potato starch stirred into 1 tablespoon water. Stir and boil until the sauce thickens. If mixture seems too thick, add a little water, stir well, and let boil briefly.

Serve with fried wontons, fried pork, fried or braised fish, cabbage, etc.

Makes 2/3 to 3/4 cup sauce
Prep and cooking time:
10 minutes

1 green onion (white part)
1 clove garlic
1 piece fresh ginger (3/4-inch section)
2 tablespoons sugar
1 tablespoon soy sauce
2 tablespoons cider vinegar
2 tablespoons rice wine
or sherry
2 tablespoons oil
2 tablespoons tomato paste
1 tablespoon potato starch
or cornstarch

[sweet and sour sauce]

True sweet and sour sauce is much more delicate and

flavorful than the sticky red sauce you find too often in

stores or restaurants. It should be a subtle blend of salty,

sour, and sweet. Chinese prefer this balance because,

they believe, the nutritional importance of a dish has more

to do with the harmony of flavors than with glucose and

fat content.

[sweet and sour fish]

Serves 4
Prep and cooking time:
35 minutes
Standing time: 15 minutes

1¼ pounds firm white
fish fillets without skin
1 piece fresh ginger (1-inch
section)
1 clove garlic
1 egg
1 cup potato starch
or cornstarch
Sweet and sour sauce
(see page 90)
Oil for frying
Salt and pepper

Rinse fish and dry with paper towels. Carefully remove all bones with clean tweezers. Cut diagonally into pieces 1-inch wide. Peel ginger and grate finely. Peel garlic and squeeze through a press. Season fish pieces with salt and pepper and rub with ginger and garlic. Let stand for 15 minutes.

Heat oil in a pot for deep-frying to 350–375°F (use an oil thermometer). Beat egg with a fork. Dip fish pieces in beaten egg, dredge in potato starch, and shake to remove excess.

Place fish in hot oil in small batches and deep-fry for 3–4 minutes, until golden brown. Drain on paper towels. Heat sweet and sour sauce and serve together while fish is hot.

[fish fritters]

Serves 4
Prep and cooking time:
30 minutes
Standing time: 30 minutes

For the batter:
1¼ cups flour
1 egg
½ cup milk
1 teaspoon baking powder

1 green onion
1 pound firm white fish
fillets without skin
3 tablespoons vermouth
Oil for frying
1 lemon
Salt and pepper

Prepare the fritter batter by combining the flour, egg, milk, and baking powder, plus a little water if necessary to obtain a liquid batter. Let stand for 30 minutes.

Peel away outer layer and chop rest of green onion. Cut fish into 1½-inch pieces. Place in a large bowl along with vermouth, green onion, salt, and pepper; stir to combine. Let stand for 20 minutes.

Heat oil for deep-frying to 350-375°F (use an oil thermometer). Dip fish pieces in batter, one by one, and brown in oil in small batches. Drain and serve very hot with lemon wedges.

Serves 6
Marinating time: at least
2 hours
Prep time: 15 minutes
Draining time: 15 minutes
Cooking time: 1 hour

4 cloves garlic
¼ cup rice wine or sherry
¼ cup soy sauce
1 tablespoon cider vinegar
1 teaspoon sesame oil
2 pounds pork spareribs
cut into 2-inch lengths (ask
butcher to do this)
3 tablespoons potato starch
or cornstarch
2 green onions
1 tablespoon five-spice
powder (see page 103)
3 tablespoons sugar
⅔ cup chicken stock
(see page 12)
Oil for frying

[five-spice spareribs]

Peel and crush garlic. Combine with rice wine, soy sauce, cider vinegar, and sesame oil. Add meat pieces and turn to coat evenly. Marinate in the refrigerator for 2 hours.

Remove pork pieces from marinade with a slotted spoon (reserve marinade) and drain on a wire rack over a platter for 15 minutes. Next, dust meat lightly with potato starch.

In a deep-fryer or pot, heat oil for frying to 350–375°F (use an oil thermometer). Fry spareribs in small batches for about 3 minutes until browned. As soon as they are done, drain on paper towels (this will get cooked more later).

Finely chop green onions and place in a wok along with marinade, five-spice powder, sugar, and chicken stock. Bring to a boil while stirring. Add meat, reduce heat, and simmer for 40 minutes, stirring occasionally. Add a little hot water if the sauce becomes too thick. Serve very hot.

stir-fried in a wok

stir-fried in a wok

the all-purpose frying pan

Even if you never make Chinese food, a wok is indispensable for cooking. It lets you fry in less oil, sear ingredients to preserve intensity of flavor, and simmer without destroying the dish's texture. When shopping for a new wok, be sure to purchase one with a cover. If you cook on an electric stove, purchase one with a slightly flattened base. The easiest to use is the nonstick type—others will last longer but may need to be seasoned, oiled, and/or cleaned in a particular way.

Serves 4–5
Prep and cooking time:
35 minutes
Soaking time: 20 minutes
Marinating time: 10 minutes

4 dried wood ear
mushrooms
4 dried shiitake mushrooms
2 duck breast fillets
2 tablespoons soy sauce
1 tablespoon potato starch
or cornstarch
1 small onion, chopped
1 clove garlic, peeled
and chopped
1 can pineapple packed
in light syrup or water
2 tablespoons oil
1 tablespoon rice wine
or sherry
$\frac{1}{8}$ teaspoon cayenne
powder (optional)
Pepper

[duck with pineapple]

Soak wood ear mushrooms and shiitakes in lukewarm water for 20 minutes. Remove skin from duck fillets and slice thinly across the grain.

Combine 1 tablespoon of the soy sauce and 1 teaspoon of the potato starch. Add chopped onion, chopped garlic, and duck slices. Stir and marinate for 10 minutes.

Drain pineapple well but save juice. Cut pineapple into smaller slices. Stir remaining potato starch into pineapple juice.

Drain mushrooms, remove/discard stems, and slice caps.

In a wok, heat oil and stir-fry duck strips over high heat for 3 minutes. Add pineapple and mushrooms and cook for 1 minute. Add pineapple juice mixture, remaining soy sauce, and rice wine. Stir, season with pepper, add cayenne if desired, and simmer for 2 minutes.

[chicken with almonds and vegetables]

Serves 4–5
Prep and cooking time:
30 minutes
Soaking time: 20 minutes
Marinating time: 10 minutes

6 dried wood ear
mushrooms
1 pound boneless skinless
chicken breast
2 tablespoons potato starch
or cornstarch
1/4 cup soy sauce
1 teaspoon sugar
1 green onion
1 bell pepper
1/2 cup bamboo shoots
2 slices prosciutto
1 1/3 cups skinless,
blanched almonds
3 tablespoons peanut oil
3 tablespoons cider vinegar
1 tablespoon rice wine
or sherry
Pepper

Soak mushrooms in lukewarm water for 20 minutes. Cut chicken into bite-size pieces. Combine 1 tablespoon of the potato starch, 2 teaspoons of the soy sauce, and sugar. Toss the chicken with this mixture and marinate for 10 minutes.

Rinse green onion and chop finely. Remove stem, seeds, and interior ribs from bell pepper; cut into strips, then into diamond shapes. Rinse bamboo shoots and cut into strips. Also, cut prosciutto into strips.

In an ungreased frying pan, toast the almonds over medium heat until lightly golden. Drain mushrooms, discard stems, and slice caps. In a wok or large frying pan, heat 2 tablespoons of the peanut oil and stir-fry chicken pieces over high heat for 2 minutes. As soon as they turn white, pour them into a strainer.

In the wok, heat remaining peanut oil and stir-fry green onion, bell pepper, bamboo shoots, mushrooms, and prosciutto for 2 minutes.

Combine remaining soy sauce, cider vinegar, rice wine, 2 tablespoons water, remaining potato starch, and pepper. Pour into the wok, return chicken to the pan, stir, and simmer for another 2 minutes. Then add toasted almonds, stir, and serve immediately.

[mongolian lamb]

Remove skin (if any present) and trim fat from lamb steaks; slice meat into bite-size pieces, against the grain. Peel garlic, squeeze through a press and combine with soy sauce, rice wine, sugar, and 1 tablespoon of the peanut oil. Add lamb pieces, stir well, and marinate for 30 minutes.
Peel onion and slice thinly. Rinse green onion, cut in half lengthwise, and then into ¾-inch stips. Cut bell pepper into strips. Peel and mince ginger.

In an ungreased frying pan, toast sesame seeds on low heat until a pale golden color (set aside). In a wok, heat remaining peanut oil and sauté onions and bell pepper strips until tender. Remove and set aside.

Stir-fry lamb in the very hot wok for 2 minutes (add more oil if necessary). Add green onions and ginger; stir-fry for 2 minutes. Add oyster sauce. Whisk stock into the potato starch, pour into the wok, and stir, cooking until sauce thickens. Return onions and bell pepper to the pan and stir for several seconds to heat through.

Pour contents of wok into a hot serving dish, sprinkle with toasted sesame seeds, and serve immediately.

Serves 4
Prep and cooking time:
30 minutes
Marinating time: 30 minutes

1½ pounds lamb leg steaks
3 cloves garlic
2 tablespoons soy sauce
2 tablespoons rice wine
or sherry
1 tablespoon sugar
2 tablespoons peanut oil
1 onion
1 green onion
¼ red bell pepper
1 piece fresh ginger
(1-inch section)
1 tablespoon sesame seeds
1 tablespoon oyster sauce
½ cup chicken stock (see
page 12)
1 teaspoon potato starch
or cornstarch

Serves 4
Prep and cooking time:
30 minutes

1¼ pounds chicken breast
1 piece fresh ginger (¾-inch section)
3 cloves garlic
1 shallot
1 small fresh red chile pepper
1 tablespoon fermented black bean sauce (Asian grocery)
¼ teaspoon sugar
2 tablespoons oil
1 tablespoon rice wine or sherry
⅓ cup chicken stock (see page 12)

[chicken with black beans]

Cut chicken breasts into bite-size pieces. Peel ginger, garlic, and shallot; chop all three finely. Remove stem and seeds from chile pepper and chop rest finely (wear gloves and don't touch your face).

Combine black bean sauce, ginger, garlic, shallot, chile pepper, sugar, and 1 tablespoon of the oil. Set aside briefly.

In a wok, heat remaining oil. Sear chicken over medium heat and stir-fry for 2 minutes. Add bean sauce mixture and continue to stir-fry for 2 minutes. Add rice wine, then the chicken stock. Bring to a boil, reduce heat, and simmer for 5–10 minutes (until chicken is cooked through and sauce is thickened). Serve very hot, accompanied by rice.

[braised eggplant]

Serves 4
Prep time: 15 minutes
Cooking time: 20 minutes

2 medium eggplant (about 1 pound total)
3 cloves garlic
2 shallots
1½ tablespoons soy sauce
1 teaspoon sugar
1 tablespoon rice wine or sherry
¼ teaspoon chile paste (Asian grocery)
1 cup chicken stock (see page 12)
3 tablespoons oil
Green part of 1 green onion (optional)

Rinse eggplant and cut into 1-inch pieces. Peel and crush garlic. Peel and chop shallots.

Combine soy sauce, sugar, rice wine, chile paste, and chicken stock.

In a wok or large frying pan, heat oil and stir-fry garlic and shallots for 1 minute. Add eggplant and stir-fry over medium heat for 2 minutes.

Add soy sauce mixture and simmer over low heat for 15 minutes. If desired, garnish with green part of green onion (sliced) and serve with rice.

[stir-fried beef with onions]

Slice meat thinly into bite-size strips. Peel and crush garlic. Peel and grate ginger. Combine beef, garlic, ginger, five-spice powder, salt, and pepper. Peel onions and slice. Combine soy sauce, sugar, potato starch, and beef stock.

In a wok, heat 1 tablespoon of the oil and stir-fry beef mixture over high heat for 2 minutes. Set aside. Wipe out wok and stir-fry onions in remaining oil over high heat for 2 minutes. Cover, reduce heat to medium, and let cook for 2 minutes.

Return beef to wok, add soy sauce-potato starch mixture, stir, and simmer gently for 1–2 minutes until sauce thickens. Serve while hot.

Serves 4–5
Prep and cooking time:
25 minutes

1 pound beef sirloin
or tenderloin
1 clove garlic
1 piece fresh ginger (¾-inch
section)
½ teaspoon five-spice
powder (see page 103)
2 onions
2 tablespoons soy sauce
2 teaspoons sugar
2 tablespoons potato starch
or cornstarch
1 cup beef stock
2 tablespoons oil
Salt and pepper

3 star anise
1 cinnamon stick (2-inch
section)
1 tablespoon Sichuan
peppercorns
1 tablespoon fennel seeds
1 tablespoon whole cloves

[five-spice powder]

Break star anise and cinnamon stick into pieces. Place all ingredients in a clean electric coffee grinder or use a clean spice mill to obtain a fine powder (to clean the grinder or mill, place white bread chunks inside and replace lid and grind—this should remove all the odors and previous contents of the grinder). Keep spice mixture tightly sealed in a small jar.

To make five-spice salt, heat 2 tablespoons salt in a very hot wok for 1 minute while stirring constantly. Remove from heat, add 2 teaspoons five-spice powder, mix thoroughly and let cool.
Keep spiced salt tightly sealed in a small jar. Serve on the side in small, individual dishes with grilled or roasted poultry.

Thanks to this hot and rapid cooking method, vegetables stay crunchy, seasonings release their aroma, and fish is never overcooked—yet all the flavors blend in perfect harmony...

[stir-fried fish with wood ear mushrooms]

Serves 4
Prep and cooking time: 30 minutes
Soaking time: 20 minutes

6 dried wood ear mushrooms
1¼ pounds fish fillets (cod, halibut, etc.)
2 tablespoons soy sauce
Several drops sesame oil
1 head Chinese (napa) cabbage
1 carrot
1 onion
1 clove garlic
⅓ cup peanut oil
Salt and pepper

Soak mushrooms in lukewarm water for 20 minutes. Rinse fish fillets, pat dry, and cut into bite-size strips. In a large bowl, combine soy sauce, sesame oil, and pepper. Add fish and marinate until needed.

Cut Chinese cabbage into strips. Peel carrot and cut into matchstick strips. Peel onion and slice thinly. Peel garlic and squeeze through a press. Drain mushrooms, remove/discard stems, and slice caps.

In a wok, heat 3 tablespoons of the peanut oil and stir-fry garlic and onion for 1 minute. Add mushrooms, carrot, and cabbage; stir-fry for 3 more minutes. Salt lightly. Transfer vegetables to a serving dish.

Heat remaining oil in the wok and sauté fish pieces for 2 minutes while stirring gently. Place on top of vegetables and serve while hot.

[stir-fried shrimp with vegetables]

Soak mushrooms in lukewarm water for 20 minutes. Remove stem and seeds from bell pepper and cut rest into small diamond shapes. Remove ends and strings from snow peas and cut diagonally into thirds. Slice celery finely. Peel and slice onion. Peel and mince garlic and ginger.

Peel and devein shrimp, rinse, and dry. Season with salt and pepper and dredge in potato starch. Drain mushrooms, remove/discard stems, and slice caps.

In a wok, heat 1 tablespoon of the oil and stir-fry garlic for 30 seconds. Add shrimp and stir-fry for 2–3 minutes until they turn pink. Add rice wine, stir, and remove shrimp.

In the wok, heat remaining oil and stir-fry ginger for 10 seconds. Add vegetables and mushrooms and stir-fry for 2 minutes. Add soy sauce, cover, and simmer for 1 minute. Return shrimp to the pan, stir, heat for 1 minute, and transfer to a serving dish. Sprinkle with almonds and serve without delay.

Serves 3–4
Prep and cooking time:
35 minutes
Soaking time: 20 minutes

3 dried shiitake mushrooms
1 red bell pepper
¼ pound snow peas
1 stalk celery
1 small onion
1 clove garlic
2 slices ginger
1 pound small shrimp
2–3 tablespoons potato starch or cornstarch
2 tablespoons oil
2 tablespoons rice wine or sherry
1 tablespoon soy sauce
1 tablespoon slivered almonds
Salt and pepper

[spinach and tofu]

Remove stems from spinach, rinse leaves, dry, and chop coarsely. Peel and mince garlic.

Heat wok, add half the spinach, and let wilt for 1 minute while stirring. Remove and wilt remaining spinach in the same way.

Wipe out the wok with a paper towel and then stir-fry garlic in hot oil for 10 seconds. Add tofu and mash it with a spatula to crumble it.

Return spinach to the pan and stir-fry for 3 minutes, then add rice wine, and simmer for another 2 minutes. Season with salt (or soy sauce) to taste.

Serves 2
Prep and cooking time:
15 minutes

1 pound spinach
2 cloves garlic
2 tablespoons oil
2 tablespoons spicy fermented tofu (Asian grocery)
2 tablespoons rice wine or sherry
Salt

[duck with bamboo shoots]

Serves 4
Prep and cooking time: 30 minutes
Soaking time: 20 minutes

8 dried shiitake mushrooms
½ cup canned sliced
bamboo shoots
2 cloves garlic
2 duck breast fillets
2½ tablespoons potato starch
or cornstarch
2 tablespoons peanut oil
¼ cup soy sauce
2 tablespoons rice wine or sherry
2 teaspoons sugar
Several drops sesame oil
Pepper

Soak mushrooms in a bowl of lukewarm water for 20 minutes. Rinse bamboo shoots and drain. Peel garlic and chop.

Remove/discard skin from duck and slice fillets crosswise against the grain. Dredge slices in 2 tablespoons of the potato starch to coat and shake off excess.

Drain mushrooms, remove/discard stems, and slice caps.

In a wok, heat 1 tablespoon of the peanut oil and stir-fry duck slices for 2 minutes. Transfer to a plate and set aside. Drain mushrooms.

Heat remaining peanut oil in the wok and add mushrooms, garlic, and bamboo shoots. Stir-fry for 30 seconds, pour in soy sauce and rice wine, sprinkle with sugar, and season with pepper. Stir remaining potato starch into 1 tablespoon water, add to wok, stir for 1 minute, and then return duck slices to the wok. Mix carefully, heating through until sauce thickens.

Add several drops sesame oil, mix again, and serve very hot.

[stir-fried pork with bamboo shoots]

Serves 4
Prep and cooking time:
35 minutes
Soaking time: 20 minutes
Marinating time: 15 minutes

4 dried wood ear
mushrooms
4 dried shiitake mushrooms
¾ pound pork tenderloin
1 tablespoon soy sauce
2 tablespoons rice wine
or sherry
1 teaspoon sugar
1 cup sliced canned
bamboo shoots
1 red bell pepper
2 shallots
2 tablespoons oil
2 tablespoons oyster sauce
1 tablespoon potato starch
or cornstarch
Salt and pepper

Soak two types of mushroom separately in lukewarm water for 20 minutes. Halve the pork tenderloin lengthwise; then, slice thinly against the grain (crosswise). Combine soy sauce, rice wine, sugar, salt, and 1 tablespoon water. Add pork, stir well, and marinate for 15 minutes.

Rinse and drain bamboo shoots. Remove/discard stem, seeds, and interior ribs from bell pepper, and cut rest into bite-size strips. Peel shallots, cut in half lengthwise, and slice thinly crosswise.

Drain mushrooms and save the soaking liquid (strain). Remove/discard stems from shiitakes. Slice caps of shiitake and wood ear mushrooms.

In a wok or large frying pan, heat oil and stir-fry shallots for 30 seconds. Add bell pepper and mushrooms and stir-fry for 2 minutes. Add bamboo shoots, pork, and bell pepper, and stir-fry for 3 minutes.

Mix together well the oyster sauce, potato starch, and a scant cup of the strained mushroom soaking liquid. Pour into the wok and stir until the sauce thickens. Serve without delay.

Heat a frying pan with a heavy base. When very hot, add salt and peppercorns and toast until the salt turns a pale golden color while shaking the pan constantly.

Pour mixture into a spice mill, salt mill, or thoroughly cleaned coffee grinder and grind to a powder. (To clean a grinder, put small chunks of white bread into it and process, then remove, and wipe out the grinder with a paper towel.)

Keep this aromatic blend tightly sealed in a jar. Serve on the side in small, individual dishes along with Asian meals.

Prep and cooking time:
10 minutes

6 tablespoons kosher or
sea salt
4 tablespoons peppercorns
(Sichuan if possible)

[salt and peppercorn blend]

How do the Chinese end their meals? Normally there isn't any dessert. Most of the time, they bring fresh fruit to the table—very ripe and carefully rinsed oranges, grapefruit, mangosteens, mangos, litchis, longans, and pears—and the host peels them one by one for all the guests. Candied fruits (ginger, coconut, lotus seeds, etc.) are also a specialty during New Year's celebrations.

[beef with oyster sauce]

Serves 4
Prep and cooking time:
30 minutes
Marinating time: 15 minutes

1 pound beef sirloin
1 tablespoon soy sauce
1 teaspoon sugar
1 tablespoon potato starch
or cornstarch
10 ounces spinach
1/3 pound fresh oyster
mushrooms
3 shallots
2 tablespoons oil
3 tablespoons oyster sauce

Cut meat into thin, 2-inch strips, against the grain. Combine soy sauce, sugar, potato starch, and meat; stir and marinate for 15 minutes. Remove/discard any tough stems from spinach, rinse very well, and pat dry (or spin to dry in a salad spinner). Slice oyster mushrooms. Peel and chop shallots.

In a wok, heat oil over high heat and stir-fry meat for 2 minutes, then remove with a slotted spoon.

Wipe out wok (leaving a thin film of oil), reheat, and add spinach, mushrooms, and shallots. Add more oil if necessary. Stir-fry over high heat for 3 minutes. Return meat to pan, pour in oyster sauce, stir to heat through, and serve.

[shrimp with a spicy sauce]

Serves 2
Prep and cooking time:
15 minutes

2 shallots
1 tablespoon soy sauce
3 tablespoons flour
1 tablespoon potato starch
or cornstarch
20 large raw shrimp
3 tablespoons ketchup
Several drops Tabasco
1 cup oil for frying
Salt

Peel shallots and chop. Combine shallots, soy sauce, 1 tablespoon water, flour, potato starch, and salt.

Peel and devein shrimp but leave the tail on. Heat oil in a wok to 350–375°F (use oil thermometer).

Dip shrimp in prepared batter and fry for 2 minutes, until lightly golden. Drain on paper towels.

Combine ketchup and Tabasco. Serve very hot fried shrimp with the sauce on the side in small, individual dishes.

Serves 5–6
Prep and cooking time:
25 minutes
Marinating time: 30 minutes
Soaking time: 20 minutes

1½ pounds beef sirloin
or tenderloin
2 cloves garlic
2 tablespoons soy sauce
6 dried wood ear
mushrooms
¾ pound snow peas
1 tablespoon rice wine
or sherry
½ cup beef stock
½ teaspoon sugar
2 teaspoons potato starch
or cornstarch
3 tablespoons oil
1 tablespoon
chopped cilantro
Salt

[stir-fried beef with snow peas]

Cut beef across the grain thinly into 2-inch strips. Peel and chop garlic. Combine beef, garlic, and soy sauce; marinate for 30 minutes. Soak mushrooms in a bowl of lukewarm water for 20 minutes.

Remove ends and strings from snow peas, cook in boiling, salted water for 3 minutes and drain. Drain mushrooms and slice.

In a small bowl, combine rice wine, beef stock, sugar, and potato starch to create the sauce. In a wok, heat 2 tablespoons of the oil and stir-fry beef over very high heat for 2 minutes, then remove.

Wipe out the wok and stir-fry mushrooms in remaining oil for 1 minute. Pour in sauce contents and stir until the mixture thickens. Return meat to the wok and add snow peas; mix well, sprinkle with chopped cilantro, and serve.

[glossary]

Chile peppers: If you don't have fresh chile peppers, you can use dried chiles, crushed red pepper flakes, hot chile oil, or any number of spicy Asian chile pastes and/or sauces.

Chinese cabbage: Various types are available, such as "napa." All types cook more rapidly than our standard, traditional cabbages. You can substitute standard cabbage in the recipes.

Chinese noodles: There are many different varieties. Wheat noodles are yellow, and rice noodles are whitish in color. Always check the package for cooking directions (length of time to be cooked or soaked in boiling water). Cellophane noodles, made from mung bean flour, swell up and become transparent when cooked.

Cilantro: Fresh cilantro is also known as Chinese parsley, or as fresh coriander leaves. It has a distinct flavor, but you can also substitute Italian parsley—it just won't be as pungent.

Ginger: Fresh ginger is a light-brown root that is easy to find. It is both fresh and spicy and can be stored at room temperature with good ventilation. Ground ginger doesn't have the same flavor and should be used in very small quantities. To use fresh ginger, first use a sharp paring knife to peel away the outer brown layer. Then either grate (or slice and mince) the remaining root.

Hoisin sauce: A thick mixture with a spicy, vinegary, and sweet flavor. You can substitute ketchup heated up and mixed with a little soy sauce.

Mushrooms: Much loved in China. Wood ear mushrooms grow on tree trunks and are also called "tree ear" or "cloud ear" mushrooms. Their flavor is mild, and they are used to provide color and texture. Shiitakes are much lighter in color and have an intense smoky flavor. Both types of mushroom are available dried. Soak them in lukewarm water for 20 minutes before using and remove/discard the (tough) stems from the shiitakes. Shiitakes are also available fresh from produce vendors, and can be sliced and stir-fried.

Oyster sauce: This thick, brown sauce is made from oyster extract, soy sauce, and brine. If necessary, you can substitute soy sauce flavored with a few drops of nuoc mam sauce (fish sauce).

Rice wine: Also known as yellow wine because of its color, rice wine has an alcohol content of 14–19% by volume. You can substitute dry sherry, which it resembles, or brandy.

Sesame oil: This oil goes well with soy sauce and is sold in small bottles. The Chinese oil is extracted from toasted sesame seeds and has a stronger flavor than the sesame oil that is generally sold in health food stores.

Shark fin: Refers to the cartilage of the dorsal and ventral fins of various species of shark. Shark fins are available dried in thin slabs (which then require a week's worth of soaking, alternating with daily sessions in boiling water) or can be purchased already prepared.

Soy sauce: Easy to find in any store. This sauce should be used sparingly—don't forget that it's very salty.

Tofu: Also known as bean curd, tofu is prepared from soybeans. Fresh tofu is smooth and white, and fried tofu has a light brown outer layer. Check the refrigerated section of your grocery store, health food stores, or Asian groceries.

[shopping tips]

Most of the products required for these recipes can be found in the international foods section of your supermarket. Some spices or obscure ingredients must be purchased in specialty stores. You will also find all types of products (noodles, rice, wonton wrappers, etc.) in Asian markets.

appendices

[index of recipes]

[table of contents]

Published originally under the title: palais chinois, © 2000 HACHETTE LIVRE (Hachette Pratique)

English translation for the U.S. and Canada © 2003 Silverback Books, Inc.

Food Editor: Kelsey Lane

Managing editors: Suyapa Audigier & Brigitte Éveno

Reader: Ann Beman

Artwork and creation: Guylaine & Christophe Moi

Production: Patty Holden & Nathalie Lautout

Assistant editor: Sophie Brissaud

Editorial office: Sylvie Gauthier

Object photography: Matthieu Csech

Cover photo: Scope / Charles Bowman

Photos: Page 10 Explorer / Y. Layma, page 32 Hoaqui / Henriette C., page 52 Scope / Charles Bowman, page 74 Pix / Didier Saulnier, page 96 Tony Stone Images / Robert van der Hilst

Printed and bound in Singapore

ISBN: 1-930603-87-8